Praise for *Becoming Who You Want to Be*

Dr. Albert Cruz has a wonderful way of explaining a new approach to time management and to moving beyond our comfort zone by writing down our goals. His metaphors explain how people need to approach their life in simple terms (even though his concepts may not be simplistic). He understands and helps people take personal action toward achieving their goals. When I finished reading his guidelines, I had an Aha moment and said to myself, "Now, I get it!" Albert's book will help me move forward, accomplishing more. If you want to move forward in your life, career, and relationships, Dr. Cruz's book is a great companion for advancement.

—**DR. SUKI STONE**, CEO, Stone Educational Systems Inc.

Albert's book provides proven guidance to all those who want to plan and live a successful life. He offers practical steps for setting comprehensive life goals and insightful guidelines for making sound decisions. Albert's own interesting real-life story is an encouragement to young people and to all immigrants to the great country of the United States.

—**DR. AMBER LO**, Retired Full Professor, National University; Author of the Chinese *Living a Tranquil and Proactive Single Life* book series

Dr. Albert Cruz, my good friend, projects such an inspirational story of his life journey since coming to America in 1983. His story, coupled with his simple guidelines and effective goal setting, can be motivational for others. Worthwhile reading to learn about his truly amazing and successful approach to life!!

—**JOHN BUGADO**, Professor Emeritus, National University

To Bonnie,
Wish best wishes!

Ashat P. Guz
2-18-2020

BECOMING WHO YOU WANT TO BE

GUIDELINES AND
GOAL SETTING FOR
AN ENRICHED LIFE

Albert P. Cruz, PhD
with **David Rytell**

ISBN-13: 978-0-9996083-8-8

Published by Albert P. Cruz
PO Box 2013, Menifee, CA 92586–1013, USA

To order, please contact book@hk2-usa.com

This publication is designed to provide accurate and authoritative information in regard to the subject matter covered. It is sold with the understanding that the publisher and author are not engaged in rendering legal, accounting, or other professional services. If legal advice or other expert assistance is required, the services of a competent professional should be sought.

Book and cover design, layout, and typesetting
    by Jan Westendorp, katodesignandphoto.com
Edited by Marial Shea
Copy-edited and proofread by Lesley Cameron
Indexed by Stephen Ullstrom
Author photo by Donald L. Carlton

Printed in Hong Kong by Regal Printing Limited
    regalprinting.com.hk

A SPECIAL THANKS TO ACANDA INTERNATIONAL LIMITED
FOR SPONSORING THIS BOOK.

To Erika Rosemary Turner, my charming,
smart, and determined granddaughter.

In loving memory of Dad,
William John Cruz (1914–1982).

CONTENTS

A Message from David Rytell

I N THE SPRING of 1997, I accepted a position at Intuit Inc., the company that made TurboTax, the popular software that makes doing your taxes simple. Arriving on my first day, I found a surprisingly large, complex operation and an office humming with activity. I was surrounded by a lot of, well, "smart people" who knew a lot of things about a lot of things. I distinctly remember being taken aback by what seemed like an unusually high number of marathon runners.

Early on, I found myself consulting with an interesting middle-aged Chinese man with glasses and the most astonishingly clean office of anyone in the entire building. His room was spick-and-span, with a simple desk, computer monitor, and keyboard—oh, and maybe he had a teacup next to that keyboard. His desk must have been wiped down too! Behind him on a counter there was only an open dictionary on a stand. But that was it. Most of the other offices had piles of papers on the desks, pencils, pens, and all kinds of knick-knacks and oddities—one office had a giant hanging pterodactyl, football trophies, and stacks of empty Diet Coke cans. (A few years later, when the occupant of this room—Albert Cruz, as I well knew by then—moved to a different part of the building, he and a few teammates made a ritual march to take his teacup, his only office possession, to the new office.)

It was immediately obvious to me that Albert was something of a different breed. Just as his immaculate office was an obvious contrast with the others in the building, he himself had an unusually sharp wit, a charming demeanor, and an amiable desire to be helpful in any way possible. And he was always funny (in his own special way). I remember thinking, "Emotional intelligence."

Albert was also well known around the office for his humorous catchphrases of wisdom. Among the first things he taught me in the cafeteria was something I was just beginning to learn in my new job: how to program computers. "When it rains, bring your umbrella," was all he said, leaning in with a whisper like it was some kind of trade secret. Then he leaned back with a satisfied look and a shrug, like, "Yeah, that's all there is to it." If you've spent time programming logic with if-statements, perhaps you can understand.

Referring again to programming, he so often offered up his helpful, time-saving technique—"Copy and paste is your friend"—that it almost became an office edict. It was Albert's way of saying, "Don't reinvent the wheel." Really, he distilled so many things down to these simple axioms that I came to think of them as Albertisms.

Occasionally, he showed me diagrams he was sketching out on the whiteboard in his office that showed a balancing of different parts of life: social, spiritual, financial, and health. He was always formulating ideas that would eventually culminate in his simple guidelines.

Soon after we first met, we began meeting up in the cafeteria for lunch each day and discussing, among other things, the issues of the day. Like his office and desk, Albert's lunch pattern was simple and predictable: lunch at 11:00 every morning, before the lunchtime crowds arrived (it's just easier), consisting of a simple homemade meal. He pointed out to me the large financial savings he had calculated from bringing his lunch every day. He was all about these kinds of simple good habits as a way of life.

At some point, we took up walking after lunch, first as a

way to aid digestion. But second, and much more important, we pledged to solve the mysteries of the universe (or at least reflect on them) during these 20-minute strolls.

This was the late 1990s. Bill Clinton was enduring scandals as president and Diana, Princess of Wales had recently died. There were a lot of issues to discuss. In technology, we were entering a time of massive change. A controversial music service called Napster was just starting out, and our own company's TurboTax was making its first ventures onto the Web. There was a lot of speculation over whether people would actually "trust" the Web enough to use a product over the Internet. The early consensus among pundits was "no." As we were in a technology-based business, these rapid advances were often a point of our discussions. We talked a lot about the Internet becoming a dominant force in the future. Things like the iPod soon appeared and, although smartphones and iPads were years away, we speculated about devices of this nature and the future effect of technology on our lives.

During those lunchtime walks, we exchanged many ideas. In our early discussions, there was plenty of talk about the impending Y2K. What would happen? On Halloween 1999, an entire wing of the Intuit offices was turned into a Y2K Haunted House, showing a brutal dystopian post-2000 world with overturned desks and chairs, flickering lights, and computer monitors flashing static.

We also talked about our personal interests. We both liked Dale Carnegie. But Tony Robbins? Too commercial. We both liked a book called The Millionaire Next Door. Financial topics were big. I talked a lot about no-load investing, Vanguard, and index funds. Albert taught me all about Warren Buffett and Berkshire Hathaway. I remember marveling that a single share of Berkshire Hathaway stock (an "A" share) was valued at about $38,000. Incredible. How far could it go? As of this writing, the same single share of Berkshire Hathaway is now valued at $274,417.

Sometimes I would pose a question, and Albert would respond with a philosophical or teaser of an answer. When many of our colleagues were making use of a generous insurance benefit for corrective laser eye surgery, and I was contemplating doing the same myself, Albert was wavering. The surgery was new, and some speculated that the short-term benefits could be offset by possible, as yet unknown, long-term drawbacks. I asked Albert what he thought I should do.

Albert answered, in a rather Socratic way, with another question: "What do Warren Buffett and Bill Gates have in common?" What?

"Of course, Warren Buffett and Bill Gates are the two wealthiest men in the world," I said after a pause.

"Yes, and what else?" he prodded.

Albert pointed out that Bill Gates and Warren Buffett are among the top five richest people in the world, with all the best experts and information, medical or otherwise, at their disposal—and they both still wear glasses. I didn't get the eye surgery.

The range of topics we discussed during our lunchtime walks was eclectic, to say the least. We talked about the recipe for Coca-Cola; the meaninglessness (to me) of Daylight Savings Time; Mozart and Chopin; and Disneyland's mysterious "secret" Club 33, a dining facility with a $10,000 membership fee to get in the door, an annual $2,000 renewal fee, and a rumored 14-year waiting list. I thought it DID exist, but maybe not. I sent a letter to Disneyland requesting an invitation, but I didn't hear anything back.

We talked a lot about high-definition TV, digital cameras, and DVDs—all of which were in the early stages of development. We talked about a future when TV might be "on demand" instead of offering only scheduled programming. We talked about a future of e-books before the Kindle or the Nook.

Sometimes I shared things from my own Western upbringing and education, like the silly intricacies of the English language or icons from pop culture, like Superman or *Star Wars*. Albert shared Chinese superstitions and parables (some of which he includes in this book). We talked about philosophy and movies too. Sometimes while we walked I talked about Stanley Kubrick films or what to look for in *Citizen Kane*. We discussed what was really meant by "Rosebud." Albert would sometimes invite my wife, Wendy, and me over to his place and screen interesting Chinese movies. One of them—a beautiful film called *Raise the Red Lantern*, starring Gong Li, a kind of Chinese Meryl Streep—became one of my all-time favorites. The film is a haunting story about a woman who becomes a concubine for a wealthy man in 1920s China and must find her place in the household hierarchy. There were English subtitles, but Albert would stop the movie from time to time to explain sections that did not translate well: the hidden meanings behind the story, the dramatic use of cinematography, or the symbolism in the film's use of color or perspective.

Really, Albert is a modest man of many surprises. Somewhere down the line, I learned that he'd been a newsreader (or anchor) in Hong Kong. Who knew?

Late in the year 2000, after I returned from a trip to New York City, we talked at length about three special buildings I had visited. One was the World Trade Center. Being uncomfortable with heights, I had decided to forgo the elevator ride to the top, but I told him how the size of the towers had been particularly startling to me. Then there was the Brown Building in Greenwich Village, the site of the terrible Triangle Shirtwaist Factory Fire in 1911 that killed more than 100 garment workers, many of whom jumped to their deaths from the high floors because they were locked in by their bosses—an unfortunate business practice at the time. Imagine the horror, we mused.

The third building, at 53rd and Lexington, the Citigroup Center, was a gigantic skyscraper in which the first nine stories are literally lifted up on huge stilts to allow St. Peter's Lutheran Church to reside underneath one of the building's corners. We also discussed how this dramatic example of modern architecture had a shocking structural flaw that had been only accidentally discovered (and subsequently retrofitted) and would have threatened total collapse under certain conditions! "Can you imagine a building collapsing in New York City?" we said. At about this same time, we talked about an Ed Bradley segment on 60 Minutes warning that it wasn't a matter of if, but when, terrorism would arrive on U.S. soil.

But most of our conversation was less weighty. Albert was always about making life meaningful—looking for and experiencing memorable things. At work, he often took groups out for dim sum, which was always enlightening. He took charge of ordering food from the carts and taught us about what we were eating by sharing the cultural meaning and history of the food. He used his "level system" to encourage guests to eat more adventurous Chinese foods—things like chicken's feet or exotic seafoods—which were sometimes too much for American tastes. If you get to "Level 1," he would say, "then your food will wink at you before you eat it!"

On one occasion, we went for lunch with a group of colleagues to what you might call a typical "American" Chinese restaurant that served things like kung pao chicken and sweet and sour pork. Like many Americans, we thought of it as Chinese cuisine, but I remember Albert saying, "This is all foreign food to me!"

We took our families to places like the Hollywood Bowl,

where we saw John Williams, and on a bus tour of celebrity homes in Los Angeles. We saw the legendary tenor Luciano Pavarotti in one of his last public appearances.

One evening, we went to a concert featuring the great cellist Yo-Yo Ma performing the Dvořák *Cello Concerto*, a signature piece for him. We sat so close—his cello was maybe 10 or 15 feet away. We later recalled hearing every nuance of that performance, including the air flowing through Ma's nostrils.

That night was September 10, 2001. Just hours later, New York City would suffer an act of terrorism that would shock the world and involve the collapse of the World Trade Center—and lead to the unimaginable horror of people jumping from the top floors to avoid burning to death.

I remember that Albert felt greatly saddened on that day as a new U.S. citizen. (Only later would I realize how much that citizenship meant to him.) So many things Albert and I had talked and thought about on our daily walks actually happened as a result of the 9/11 attacks that I have often thought of discussions with Albert as being uniquely insightful and even prophetic.

When it came time for Albert to leave Intuit and pursue his dreams in academia, he performed a final ritual. He took his few things (there wasn't much, but I remember the teacup) and insisted on discreetly walking out of the company's front door instead of the side door we always took to the parking lot. He always wanted to commemorate an occasion symbolically. This time he wanted to exit the way he'd first come in and to symbolically close the door behind him as he moved on to his next endeavor.

Albert had a list of things he wanted to do, and it was now time for him to get busy. I'd already seen the sign at the foot of the driveway of his first home that said "The First Step," and inside he had made a bar with beer on tap because he'd "always wanted one." Now he wanted not just a degree, but a master's and a PhD. He wanted to teach. He wanted to someday write a book.

About 10 years after Albert stepped out the front door of Intuit, we would find our way into Club 33 at Disneyland, albeit as guests and not members. Disneyland had finally answered my letter with an invitation, and with who else but Albert would I want to go? We had a great time dining in the club—and in 1901, the sister club in California Adventure Park—but we both agreed membership wasn't our game. By then the dues were a little higher: $30,000 to join and $10,000 per year.

Today we remember our years at Intuit, and those daily walks, fondly. We appreciate the productive and interesting times and recall with regret our friends from those years who are no longer with us.

As you read Albert's story, I think you'll recognize his sense of ritual mixed in with his unique sense of humor and wisdom. This is his nature. You would be wise to pick up a few habits from him. I still eat lunch at 11:00 a.m. today, because, well, it's just easier.

In the pages that follow, Albert has a thoughtful story to tell about his journey to the U.S.A. from Hong Kong. It's about the immigrant experience and about working overtime to achieve a life of balance and satisfaction. Albert's story and the Nine Simple Guidelines he developed can help distill life down to its essence: simple, logical steps toward ultimate goals.

Remember, "if it rains . . . bring your umbrella."

—DAVID RYTELL
NOVEMBER 2017
LA MESA, CALIFORNIA

Preface

I STRONGLY BELIEVE in knowledge sharing. The main motivation for me to write this book was to inspire you, my readers, by sharing my life experiences, the guidelines I have developed and followed over the past half century, and the goal-setting method I designed. The guidelines have steered me toward becoming the person I want to be, while the goal-setting method has given me a clear and organized structure for working toward and achieving my goals. Together, they have greatly helped me live a successful and enriched life.

My original idea was to simply present my guidelines and goal-setting method in two parts. But upon reflection, I realized that the reader might benefit from knowing a little about the experiences from which I developed these tools. This is how my book came to have three parts.

Part One records the events and challenges I encountered after immigrating with my family to the United States in 1983. It was these very challenges that inspired me to adopt and refine the Nine Simple Guidelines for an Enriched Life, elaborated in Part Two, and to further develop Effective Goal Setting: A Balanced Approach, described in Part Three.

If you want to get right to the heart of this book, you can skip to Part Two and learn about the guidelines I have lived by. There, you will also read many stories about my formative years in Hong Kong, when I embarked on my search for the most effective ways to achieve success in life and business. As part of that search, I began to collect ideas and concepts that I then tested, adopted, and applied to crucial situations.

If you are interested in the mechanics of designing balanced goals, fast-forward to Part Three.

Throughout my life, I have benefited from wisdom and experience generously shared by others. I have therefore made every attempt here to credit the sources of quotations and concepts that have helped me become the person I want to be.

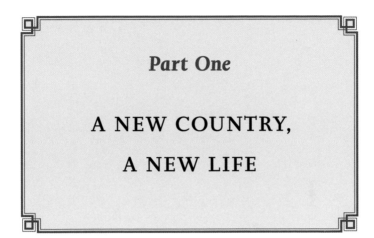

Part One

A NEW COUNTRY, A NEW LIFE

Introduction
1982 to Present

MY MIDLIFE CRISIS was real and tough. At age 38, I gave up all I had to start a new life in a foreign country. In 1984, shortly after I arrived in California, I felt like I was falling into a deep hole. It was murky down there, and when I tried to pull myself out, the walls were slippery. Every time I tried to climb up, I fell right back down. I could not move any higher, because I could barely stand.

Before I could become the person I wanted to be, I had to stand up to the challenges of a different culture, of making a living without sufficient education or any connections. In short, I had to take back control of my life. "Being able to stand" was an important metaphorical objective. This is why, eight years later, I would name the very first single-family house I bought *The First Step*. This purchase was a noteworthy milestone, signifying that I had finally taken my first significant footstep in my new life and was finally moving forward.

During what I call my transition and hardship years, I was extremely fortunate. "When the going gets tough," they say, "the tough get going." And I did get going. In many "tough" situations, I was able to turn things around for the better. As a result, not only did I quickly pull myself out from that deep hole, but I was able to climb even higher. The graph that best describes the progress of my years in California looks like a J-shaped curve—sliding down initially, turning back up swiftly, and finally rising higher and higher.

This first part of the book is about how I weathered the transition years, survived the hardship years, settled down in the accomplishing years, and continue to enjoy the freedom years.

1. Transition Years
1982 to 1983

Leap, and the net will appear.
—JOHN BURROUGHS

A PHONE CALL on February 10, 1982, triggered a chain of events that would alter the course of my life. It was my mom calling from San Diego, across 7,000 miles of ocean, to say that my dad had died—suddenly and unexpectedly—of a heart attack. He was only 67.

Reeling from shock and disbelief, I took the long flight from Hong Kong to California to take care of the funeral arrangements. My last conversation with Dad had been fewer than 10 days earlier, when I called him from Tokyo, Japan, where my family and I had experienced the magic of our first snowfall. Fond memories of my time with Dad circled around me during the tiring and anxious 20 hours of travel.

In 1975, Dad retired from the United States Navy, where he'd served as a Deputy Disbursing Officer, the highest local civilian grade. He had been one of the few foreign nationals appointed in Hong Kong. That same year, he and Mom decided to immigrate to the United States, eventually settling in San Diego. The following year, I took my first trip to the United States. My employer, Sentry Insurance Hong Kong, a subsidiary of an American company, sent me to Oshkosh, Wisconsin, to attend a workshop and then visit its headquarters at Stevens

Point. In addition to visiting my parents, I had the opportunity to stop over in a few other cities in the U.S. I was thrilled by the vastness of the country and the dynamic people I met.

Yet, the thought of moving to the United States never entered my mind. Within eight years, I had progressed from being an insurance agent with ManuLife to being Sales and Marketing Vice President of Sentry Insurance Hong Kong, and then founding my own insurance services firm, Acanda International Ltd., in 1978. My clientele was growing and my revenue increasing steadily. I enjoyed the freedom of running my own company. Why would I want to give up this freedom and success and my connections with close relatives, friends, and clients?

One day, however, breaking news totally disrupted my status quo.

Decision and Preparation to Emigrate to the U.S.A.

In a moment that foreshadowed the future of Hong Kong, on September 24, 1982, Margaret Thatcher, then prime minister of the United Kingdom, slipped and stumbled while descending the steps of the Great Hall of the People in Beijing, China. The awkward scene was caught on camera and replayed many times in Hong Kong. She had just come from a meeting with Chairman Deng in which she was told that China would unilaterally announce its policy to retake Hong Kong if no agreement was reached within two years.[1] Over the next year, the Hong Kong stock market tumbled 38 percent, and its currency devalued a record 42 percent against the U.S. dollar.

This latest political conflict between the British and Chinese governments about the future of Hong Kong sparked a question in my mind: Is it still in my family's best interests to be in Hong Kong? Emigration had been the talk of the town for quite a while. For me, China's most recent pronouncement was the last straw. On that very day I made up my mind. We would leave Hong Kong—for good.

Soon after, I brought out my three-ring binder that held detailed records of the balanced goals I had set up and followed since 1975 (see more about goals in Part Three). I crossed out many of my short- and medium-term goals. My life goals would need to be completely remapped.

I asked Mom to file a petition to bring my family and me to the United States as permanent residents. She hired an attorney to help her file the forms. After many long-distance phone calls and much paperwork, we were told to wait. I assumed we would have to wait many years, giving us plenty of time to prepare for our move. But it turned out there was no waiting period for the married children of U.S. citizens born in China. Surprisingly, a petition acceptance arrived from the United States Consulate in Hong Kong in the summer of 1983. I still recall my mixed feelings of sadness and excitement when I took the letter from my post office box. We instantly began our preparations for leaving the British colony of Hong Kong.

Family history was repeating itself. Nearly 40 years earlier, in 1946, my parents had brought me, still a baby, to Hong Kong from Shanghai, China, because of the unstable political climate, shortly before the Chinese Communist Party took power. Now, in 1983, with the impending changeover of the government and the instability and uncertainty that this changeover threatened, my wife, Teresa, and I believed staying was too politically risky for our two young daughters.

So, the decision to begin a new life was prompted by two mental forces: push and pull. One push was the perceived untrustworthiness of the future Hong Kong government administration. I did not have confidence in the proposed *one country, two systems* under which Hong Kong would become a Special Administrative Region (of the People's Republic of China), with its own legal system, currency, and freedom of the media (*Really?*). A further push was the increasingly crowded and polluted living conditions in Hong Kong.

The pull was that Mom was living by herself and getting older. I wanted my family to be closer to her. Moreover, we were going to live in the finest city of the *greatest* country in the world. Yay!

Even with these powerful attractive forces, moving to a place over 7,000 miles away was a huge project and a logistical nightmare. In preparation for the big move, I compiled a list of action items that became part of my updated short-term goals.

It wasn't all work, however. One of my goals was for my family and me to visit as many popular local spots as we could around Hong Kong Island, Kowloon, and the New Territories before we left. I wanted us to see any attractions that might not be the same, or might even be gone, when and if we ever returned.

While it was important to me that we have some fun together, I included this action item for more than just amusement. I also value completion in everything I do, something I learned in my teens from my calligraphy teacher. When I disliked the way I had started a character and wanted to start over, my teacher would scold me: "Always finish what you start. If you want to cross out a character because you don't like your work, you must finish it first." I wanted to bring full completion to this era of our lives and to celebrate our homeland before leaving it.

Along with visiting local attractions, we patronized many restaurants serving diverse authentic ethnic dishes, tasting provincial cuisines from Beijing, Chaozhou, Guangdong, Haka, India, Shanghai, Taiwan, and more. We had a blast!

U.S.A., Here We Come!

On December 19, 1983, after presenting our immigration papers during a brief layover in Seattle, we arrived in San Diego. For me, it was the same long flight as a year before, but this time the trip was full of uneasiness rather than sadness. For the first time in my life, I was stepping into uncharted territory. The future was foggy. My only certainty was that, from that day forward, my life would never be the same.

At the San Diego International Airport, we were heartily greeted by a welcoming party. Mom was at the arrivals gate with her dear friends Thurman, Warren, and Clarke, three American brothers, all sporting Santa Claus hats and a big "welcome" banner. The three brothers, all retired military, had been giving their generous help and support to Mom while she was by herself. Our fatigue from the long journey was instantly eradicated by their cheers.

The First Few Weeks

Shortly after our arrival, friends of ours from Hong Kong who had arrived in San Diego one year earlier, Connie and Julius, invited us to their home for our very first Christmas dinner in the United States. It was quite a feast, with plenty of fresh salad and roast rib of beef, a rare commodity in Hong Kong. (Fresh imported beef was available mostly to caterers, not consumers, in Hong Kong.) Our youngest daughter, Mary-Ann, got acquainted that day with Winnie, their daughter of a similar age. Mary-Ann and Winnie remain the closest of friends.

Later that week, Connie and Julius took us to several model home tours nearby. We were overwhelmed by the gorgeous and spacious designs and the aesthetics of the surrounding landscape. What a contrast to the small apartment unit in the high-rise concrete building where we grew up.

Mom's Mexican friend, Fred (a colleague of Dad's), took us south of the border on a day trip to Tijuana. His remarkably warm personality impressed the whole family. He even taught me a few phrases in Spanish. A few days later, he introduced us to a membership-only store, Price Club (now Costco). We were fascinated by its vastness and the astonishing variety of products. It was quite a magnificent sight to behold. What a concept!

However, I wanted to get down to business as soon as possible. An insurance associate in Hong Kong had referred me to Don Goode, a San Diego broker. I called him the day after I arrived, and he came by right away to Mom's house, where we were staying. Don drove me to his office in his Ferrari—my first ride in such a nice car. He provided me with a huge amount of helpful information. My plan was to start an insurance business, and the first step was to take a test to get my insurance license. Don gave me the study materials for the test and even gave me a map book showing all the local streets.

Later that week, Don picked Teresa and me up in his RV—the inside space was nearly as much as you'd find in a mini apartment in Hong Kong, but this house could move! He took us to our very first football game, at Jack Murphy (now Qualcomm) Stadium, which included a spectacular fireworks display during half-time. It was the 1983 Holiday Bowl, BYU versus Missouri. A touchdown by Steve Young, with just 23 seconds left, gave BYU a 21–17 win. The atmosphere and excitement were stunning. It was a jaw-dropping experience for me, because I had never attended any event on such a grand scale. Over the following months, Don also took me to a San Diego Sockers game at the Sports Arena and to the San Diego Police Pistol Range to fire a *real* gun. Wow!

Throughout my early struggling years, both Don and his son and business associate, Phil, went above and beyond in helping me launch and build my insurance business. Phil showed me around the business districts in San Diego and took me to many car dealerships, helping me buy my very first car from an auto broker. A brand-new car was delivered to the parking lot of my apartment, because I did not yet know how to drive.

One day in the second week of our arrival, Mom's friend Thurman took us to apply for our social security cards. The Social Security Administration Office was in the downtown federal building, near the impressively beautiful San Diego Harbor, one of the world's finest natural harbors, along with Hong Kong. Dad once told me that watching San Diego Harbor in the evening, with the reflected lights from the buildings across Shelter Island, reminded him of Hong Kong's Victoria Harbor.

While we were at the federal building, we passed by another federal government department. Thurman said jokingly, "On behalf of the Internal Revenue Service, welcome to America."

Little did I know that in 10 years I would be analyzing tax form instructions and the U.S. Internal Revenue Code to develop tax preparation software, and that I would become an enrolled agent of the IRS (a person who has earned the privilege of representing taxpayers before the IRS).

At this point, so soon after our arrival, my mind was already overloaded with all the many new adventures, concepts, and sights. I felt I needed time to digest everything I had seen, heard, and done. We were deeply touched by the kindness and cordiality of the American people in welcoming us to our new country. Within a few weeks of settling down, my family and I were being helped with our basic living needs by Thurman, Warren, and Clarke; Connie and Julius; Fred and his wife, Angie; Don and Phil; Joan (a friend Mom met at church); and Dede (Mom's next-door neighbor). They helped us find and rent an apartment, set up utility services, buy furniture and a car, and find schools for our daughters, Janette and Mary-Ann. They drove us around before I got my driver license and familiarized us with some local tourist attractions. One of them served as my reference when I applied for my very first credit card in the United States.

We could not thank these friends enough for their generosity and compassion. Thanks to their help, I felt prepared to face the challenges ahead. Experience told me I would not be afraid of doing things that made me feel uncomfortable—I always liked to try something new and different. Even though the challenges I would be facing were larger than any I had ever confronted, I knew I would not give up without a fight (see "Walking toward is better than walking away," on page 91).

With that, I stepped determinedly into the early spring of 1984. At age 39, I was facing a new beginning. The pressing question: Was I ready?

2. Hardship Years
1984 to 1991

Success is failure turned inside out –
The silver tint in the clouds of doubt,
And you never can tell how close you are,
It might be near when it seems afar;
So stick to the fight when you're hardest hit –
It's when things seem worst that you must not quit.

—ANONYMOUS

To say I had to learn nearly everything from scratch in my first year as an immigrant would be quite an understatement. Everything was just a bit overwhelming. The culture, traditions, customs, slang, system of government, and most distinctly, the sheer vastness of the landscape—everything felt strange. Once the honeymoon was over, I wasn't certain I was ready to begin my re-education, and honestly, I wasn't entirely aware I needed it. But ready or not, the process of relearning proved to be both frustrating and eye-opening.

I remember the first time I drove with my family north on Interstate 5 from San Diego to San Francisco. My youngest daughter, Mary-Ann, woke up after a long nap. Noticing we had been on the road for over six hours, she asked me if we had left the United States. My other daughter, Janette, looked at her and laughed. I assured Mary-Ann that we were still in California and thought, "My baby frog has just climbed out from a narrow well and seen a much grander open sky."

Prior to the move, my life was mostly confined to within the relatively tiny perimeter of the Kowloon Peninsula (where I lived) and the Island of Hong Kong (where I worked), a total space of less than 50 square miles. It absolutely blew my mind to think that the land size of San Diego County alone is over 4,500 square miles—90 times the area I was used to.

A Taste of the California Lifestyle: Driving

When I lived in Hong Kong, I did not feel any need to learn to drive. There was an efficient public transportation system and destinations inside the highly congested metropolitan city were close. But within days of my arrival in Southern California, I realized that owning a car and knowing how to drive were essential. I had to learn to drive—and quickly. But first I needed to get access to a car. So, I did something rather unusual: I bought my first car before I knew how to drive.

One day, with a visiting relative sitting next to me, I took control of a brand-new Nissan Sentra. It was literally the first time I had ever sat in the driver's seat, and of course, I was nervous. So many gears to get to know, a dashboard crowded with meters, an accelerator pedal, brake pedal, gear shift, seat belt, and rear-view and side mirrors. (*Wait! You mean I should watch the road too?*)

I switched on the engine, and my subconscious took over, pulling me over to the left side of the road, where we drive in Hong Kong. Within minutes of my first driving practice beginning, I had a near head-on collision! Though this was quite a scary moment for my passenger, the driver of the other car, and me, that driver was—luckily—a nice lady. She just honked.

After a few days of practice, I took my first road test. I failed. A week later, after several more hours of practice, I failed again, and felt disappointed and embarrassed. It was not until I signed up for professional driving school and went through proper training that I was finally able to score my California driver license. Learning to drive from a professional turned out to be a good decision. The skills I gained would prove invaluable (see "Actively seeking knowledge is better than passively receiving it," on page 135). I have been a safe and accident-free driver since.

A Taste of American English

Hong Kong was a British colony during the whole time I lived there. English was an official language, and remained so after the change of government. I was brought up learning to speak both Cantonese and English. Cantonese is used in daily social interactions, but English is used in schools, commercial dealings with Westerners, and all government communications. I thought I knew English before I came to San Diego. What I didn't realize was that many words and phrases were used in America in a different (sometimes very different) way than I was accustomed to. I found myself having to learn this new, American form of English.

For instance, instead of lift, Americans say *elevator*; instead of *rubbish*, they say *trash*. *Cool* commonly means *excellent* or *very good*, or is used to express agreement with what someone has said. *Bad* sometimes means *good*. The first floor of a building is its *ground* floor. A *duplex* consists of two attached houses instead of a *two-story* unit in a high-rise residential building. A *spanner* is called a *wrench* here, and you fill up your car at a *gas*, not a *petrol*, station. When Americans said *hot*, it sounded to me like *hard*, and I wondered why I was being warned that the coffee was "hard." When they said *heart*, I thought they meant *hot*, and I couldn't hear much difference between *can* and *can't*.

Not everyone who tried to school me in my new culture actually succeeded. An insurance agency office clerk once attempted to correct my grammar when I asked for a clause to be added to an insurance policy with the words "its successors and or assigns."

"The possessive pronoun of it should be *it's* not *its*," said the clerk, and insisted that I change the word before the policy endorsement request was sent to the insurance company.

"But, *it's* is the contraction for *it is* or *it has*," I said.

"Do you think your English is better than mine?"

But really, I was having fun relearning the English language. I remember what turned out to be a hilarious incident when I was shopping for my first car. One day during the second week after our arrival, when I was still suffering from the 16-hour time difference, Teresa and I went to a car dealership.

As soon as we entered the car lot, we were excitedly welcomed by a grinning salesperson. Our conversation went something like this:

"Morning, folks. Welcome. How ya doin'?"

I was tired and a bit timid, but I said, "We are interested in getting a new car."

After glancing at Teresa, he turned to me and said, "Hmm . . . it must be a first car for your pretty daughter here. Congratulations! I'll be happy to assist you." Now his smile was even bigger.

I guessed it was hard for most Americans to estimate the age of Asian women.

He then turned to Teresa and asked her, "Which model and color are you looking for? I can give you a *really* excellent price."

I spoke softly to the salesperson. "She is not my daughter. She is my wife!"

He glared at us, feigning a serious look.

"*Get outta here!*" he said.

And so, being new to this "American-style" humor, we left!

As we were walking away, I uttered to Teresa, "How rude!" It took me a few years to realize that "get outta here" was a slang expression and should not be taken literally. Really, the salesperson was complimenting Teresa. What an interesting use of an English phrase!

And so, on top of all my other lessons in this new American English, I learned that we might not really need to leave when someone says, "Get out of here!"

A Taste of Culture Shock

Throughout this period of adaptation, I also had to learn how to cope with culture shock, directions, food, and systems of measurement. Let's look at those one at a time.

A popular Chinese golden rule tells us, yī shí zhù xíng (the four basic needs of life in the order of importance are: clothing, food, shelter, and transportation). The Chinese rank dressing properly higher than the other three because how one looks is a status symbol, and therefore more important than what one eats, let alone where one lives. The least important is how one commutes. (The Chinese character xíng could also mean walking or moving around.)

In California, the rankings are reversed, with transportation first, then shelter, followed by food, and finally clothing. It seems that here in the U.S., one must have the means to commute and a home address to arrive at before one can seek employment to put food on the table. With some exceptions, dressing well seems to be least important.

As a case in point, many of my colleagues at the community college where I teach come to school meetings dressed in T-shirts, shorts, and sandals, especially in the summer. This would be unimaginable in Hong Kong, where most professionals adhere to British dress codes. A suit and tie are considered proper attire, with a minimum standard of business casual at a school or college.

Every small cultural nuance was new. It was like reinterpreting and relearning simple, daily functions one by one. From time to time, I struggled to pick up the subtle cultural differences of nonverbal communication. Americans are more outspoken and open-minded, with more explicit facial expressions, than Chinese people. I saw plenty of smiling faces everywhere I went. I felt a bit awkward when a total stranger said "Hi" to me. Hugging someone who is not close is acceptable here. Splitting checks at a restaurant is common. Calling parents, bosses, and teachers by their first names is not being disrespectful. (I have even received emails from students that open with "Hey, prof . . ." *Really!*)

And literally finding my bearings was a challenge. In stark contrast to my previous life of crisscrossing just a few major thoroughfares in Hong Kong, navigating around San Diego County was daunting. It took me a long time to work out that west is toward the ocean and east is toward the mountains. East–west routes are assigned even numbers. North is going up to Los Angeles, south is down to Mexico. North–south routes are assigned odd numbers. I was thrilled by the dynamics of the gigantic interstate freeway system. And, oh yes, a right turn on a red light is allowed in California! Of course, I would turn only after a complete stop and when it was clear.

But When the Going Gets Tough, the Tough Go *Restaurant Hopping!*

Teresa has always been known for her superb home cooking. Her extensive cooking skills include mastery of many popular cuisines not only from different Chinese cities but also from other countries. However, with not being able to buy authentic ingredients, she could prepare few Chinese dishes during our early months in San Diego. Soon after our initial excitement over American foods (*What are those?*), we grew tired of pizza, hamburgers, and fried chicken, though we continued to enjoy fresh green salads. We also missed our customary weekly social gatherings with friends and relatives in restaurants back in Hong Kong.

Throughout those first years, we would occasionally have strong cravings for authentic Chinese cuisine. We felt homesick and looked for comfort food, but the availability of Asian groceries was limited at best in San Diego. (It's a different story today.) Many local Asian restaurants offered American-style Chinese dishes such as chop suey and chow mein (*Without noodles, are you kidding me?*). In Cantonese, *chow* means fry or fried and *mein* means noodle. Thus, *chow mein* in Hong Kong is fried noodles. Not so in San Diego. Coping with eating these strange types of foods was not easy.

We longed for the real thing—and I don't mean Coca-Cola—and so found ourselves driving 120 miles to Old Chinatown in Los Angeles to experience the once-familiar smells of wok-fried cooking, to hear the hum of many people chitchatting, to taste the delicious flavors of dim sum (bite-sized portions of Cantonese cuisine), and to see the carts filled with familiar treats circling among the narrow spaces between the tables. While we were in Chinatown, we also went to the Asian markets to stock up on Chinese vegetables, tea leaves, and Cantonese-style *char siu* (barbecue pork) and *siu ngap* (Cantonese-style roast duck)—yummy!

U.S. versus Metric System of Measurement

When I was a primary school student, I was taught what was known in the British Empire as the imperial system of measurement. In my arithmetic class, it was particularly hard to work on calculation problems involving the old British monetary system in which 12 pennies equaled one shilling and 20 shillings equaled one pound. During my high school years, the government of Hong Kong switched over to the metric system of measurement. I had to change my assessments of weight, distance, and temperature to kilograms, kilometers, and Celsius.

Once I was in the United States, I had to essentially change back to the imperial system. It was quite awkward when I had to fill in my height and weight on a form, because I had no idea what those numbers were in feet, inches, and pounds. I don't understand why imperial measurement is still used in the United States.

Running into Financial Difficulties

Along with re-education, I also had to establish a credit rating and look for an income-producing activity.

As a new immigrant with no credit history, I had a tough time getting a credit card or a mortgage. During the early months, a salesperson from a major retail store persuaded Teresa and me to apply for a store credit card after Teresa made some purchases. Within a week, I received a notice that our application had been denied, without explanation. I had never had a credit application turned down before. It was a great disgrace, and I felt hurt. I had been doing well financially in Hong Kong. I soon realized that establishing and keeping good credit, so vital to my financial well-being in the United States, wouldn't be as easy as I'd thought.

With no U.S. credit history, I was forced to pay cash deposits when I applied for utility services, I had to have a guarantor to cosign my residential lease agreement, and I had a tough time getting car insurance.

Setting Up My Own Insurance Services Firm

After high school, I entered the field of insurance sales and services. Having started my own insurance services firm a few years prior to my emigration, I naturally planned on setting up a similar business in San Diego.

It didn't take long to discover my efforts were going nowhere. I felt like I was constantly hitting a brick wall, even with the help of a lot of people, including Don and Phil; Thurman, Warren, and Clarke; and Connie and Julius. As much as I wanted to use my experience and ability to start a new U.S. business, the playing field here was completely different. My lack of connections made it extremely difficult to find clients. Though I was trying hard to make ends meet, I began to doubt if my business was even workable.

Almost daily, I had to deal with problematic clients, non-supportive insurance agency staff, and demanding insurers. One insurer even ended my contract unilaterally and would not pay me any future residual commissions due to the lack of business. I was very upset and angry at myself for being so helpless (see "Responding is better than reacting," on page 113).

But, When the Going Gets Tough, the Tough Go *Driving!*

I found that long-distance freeway driving, with soft music playing in the background, would always ease my depression and desperation. I decided to see more of the cities in the region.

We would occasionally drive up to San Francisco, where I explored the potential for prospective insurance clients in the Bay Area and visited Dominic (a buddy of my brother Tom) and a high school buddy, Gary, and his family. Gary was the first among my closest friends to come to the United States. He moved to Tucson in the early 1960s and later settled in San Francisco. Gary has always been an easy-going and generous guy, and I was fortunate to reconnect with him. Gary's wife, Emily, introduced us to her sister, Betty, who lived in Cerritos, a suburb of Los Angeles.

Betty and her husband, Raymond, had come to California from Hong Kong a few years before us. They also had two very young daughters, Winnie and Lindsey. We spoke the same dialect, were of a similar age, and shared a lot of interests. My wife and I drove to Cerritos almost monthly to spend the weekends with them, and our families quickly became very close. They were such a generous and caring couple. Every meal we had at their house was a feast.

Betty and Raymond introduced me to many new friends, a few of whom even became my insurance clients. What I appreciated most about them, especially during my hardship years, was that they never looked down on us. They made my family feel accepted. Getting together with them helped alleviate our homesickness during our early settling years. For a number of years, our two families explored many places all over Southern California and Mexico together. We visited Huntington Library, La Brea Tar Pits, Solvang, SeaWorld, La Jolla, Tijuana, and Puerto Nuevo, to name only a few.

There is a great advantage to living in a country with a vast landscape. My new home city of San Diego, with its location and huge size, allowed me the convenience of easy access to many diverse climates. The ocean, the desert, and mountains are all within about an hour's drive. In December, one could easily drive through all four seasons within a day. Places such as San Francisco, Phoenix, Tucson, Las Vegas, and Laughlin are all within a day's drive. Whenever I had time off, I explored many of those cities. For me, traveling was truly educational. It opened my mind to the environment and led me to experience exciting adventures. Although I missed some of Hong Kong's fast-paced, dynamic city lifestyle, I would never have visited such a variety of interesting places had I stayed there.

With all these long road trips, I was putting a lot of mileage on the car. Having never owned a car before, maintenance was a totally new concept for me. Often, when I brought my car to a mechanic for servicing—simple oil changes, most of the time—I was told there were more, often critical repairs needing immediate attention. I wondered how often a car needs a transmission flush, wheel alignment, and replacement of timing belts. My clueless look and lack of knowledge might have given the mechanic some hints that I was a sucker. In 1985, I had to pay $900 (equivalent to $2,000 in 2017) to have a radiator coolant leak repaired. That unexpected payment inflicted a tremendous burden at a time when my income was low. But I had no choice. San Diego's public transit system was not efficient enough for my work in sales. I needed to drive. Very quickly, out of necessity, I learned quite a bit about car maintenance.

But, When the Going Gets Tough, the Tough Go *Instructing!*

During my late teens and early twenties, I experienced two emotionally disturbing incidents that would cast a shadow over my self-esteem for years to come. My first step toward turning my life around was reading Dale Carnegie's books, which led me to Dale Carnegie Training.

Taking this well-known communications and human relations course is what enabled me to finally put down the negative mental baggage I had been carrying for years and regain my self-confidence. Course activities and the interactions between class members inspired me to trust myself and recognize that *it was up to me to run my life.*

The Dale Carnegie instructors appreciated my enthusiasm and invited me to participate in the course many times as a graduate assistant. Not only did I learn a great deal about the structure and background of the course, I was also awakened to life's rich possibilities by listening to many more talks by class members.

Eventually, I completed a rigorous instructor training program and qualified as an instructor myself. I remember teaching many weekend classes with Michael Cheung in a drug rehabilitation center on Shek Kwu Chau, an isolated island in Hong Kong that was closed to the public.[2] (Michael later became the local sponsor of Dale Carnegie Courses.) We needed to tandem-teach the brand-new Cantonese version of the course before offering it to the public, and we would spend the night on the island because the ferry service was very limited. One of the talks from that island was recorded in a revised edition of *How to Win Friends and Influence People*.[3]

Over eight years, I taught many classes, both in Cantonese and in English, doing my best to give back to my class members what I had received: motivation to become more effective in their personal lives and regain their self-confidence. A few of them would later become best friends I still hold dear after four decades.

Along with Dale Carnegie Training, I also took other self-improvement courses, read books, and attended many motivational talks. I was searching wholeheartedly for the best way to live. I started keeping notes and posting them where I would see them every day—notes I would eventually distill into my nine guidelines and the balanced approach to goal setting I present in Parts Two and Three.

Years later, when I was struggling to settle into my new life in San Diego, I thought about all the positive teachings I'd learned from Dale Carnegie Training. One day within a few months of my arrival, I found myself wondering if a Dale Carnegie course was offered in San Diego. I found a local manager, and called him to introduce myself. One thing led to another. After going through a vigorous recertification training and tandem-teaching with another instructor for several courses, I was privileged to resume instructing in San Diego. Never in my wildest dreams did I think I would be involved with my favorite self-improvement course again, but here I was.

The structure of a Dale Carnegie course includes two two-minute talks given by each class member in each weekly session. Within a year, as a facilitator, I had listened to over a thousand talks. There can be no better way to get to know the local culture (and slang as well as facial expressions) so quickly and in such vivid detail. Within a few years I had developed a cordial bond with the manager, the staff, my fellow instructors, and many class members. I continued to teach the course for seven years in San Diego, El Centro in Imperial County, and Rancho Cucamonga in San Bernardino County.

Going to nearby cities during the weekends and teaching courses on weekday evenings infused me with a great deal of positive energy. This helped me keep my positive attitude—despite the frustration I felt about my failing insurance services business.

A Bitter Taste of Hopelessness

In spite of my considerable efforts to get new clients, my insurance services business was simply going nowhere. Eventually, I had to close it down because the income was insufficient to cover taxes and expenses, let alone bring money home.

Truthfully, there were times when I had serious doubts about having come to the United States. But in the rare moments when I thought of going back to Hong Kong, I felt too proud to return as a failure (see "Walking toward is better than walking away," on page 91). Still, at that time I had no idea what options there were for me. With my lack of work experience in America and just a foreign high school education, I could not imagine what I might do.

I did earn some extra cash from teaching Dale Carnegie courses and receiving dividends from my Hong Kong company, but my expenses were continually exceeding my income. As my bank balance fell to a dangerously low level, I began to worry whether or not I could survive financially. I realized that I needed additional income.

But, When the Going Gets Tough, the Tough Go *Seeking Additional Income!*

One day, a business associate recommended that I contact a temporary work agency. He told me that if I could prove I could legally work in the United States, I should be able to earn some income. I went to an agency office, filled out a couple of forms, and handed over all the required documents. When the interviewer asked me to take a typing test (using an *electric* typewriter), I felt a bit humiliated. Back in Hong Kong, I always had my own personal secretary to type all my business and personal letters. The wages and status of a typist were among the lowest in any organization. (*Will I be hired as a typist?*) Anyway, I followed the instructions and typed a short page. Having taken typing in high school, I believed I did well. At the end of the interview, I was told to wait for calls.

Not too long after, I got my first assignment—making five dollars an hour at a local Sony electronics factory in the upscale community of Rancho Bernardo. Upon arrival, I was told by a supervisor that my job would be screwing speakers onto the television sets as they slowly passed by on a conveyor belt. That reminded me of the factory scene from Charlie Chaplin's *Modern Times*. That was all I did for eight hours. To say the least, it was a very boring job. I told myself that if that was what I had to do to make a living, my life was screwed—literally. (Twenty years later, I would experience an interesting *reversal of misfortune* when I bought a brand-new 3,100-square-foot home with *cash* in the very same community, within a short distance of the Sony factory.)

A second assignment came soon afterward from the same electronics factory. I was to report to a hotel in Mission Bay, unload boxes from a truck onto a dolly, and push them to a hall where the factory was hosting a corporate function. Pushing that dolly, I rolled through my past in my head. Back in Hong Kong, I had been the Sales and Marketing Vice President of Sentry Insurance Hong Kong, a subsidiary of an American corporation. I then founded an insurance services firm and enjoyed a decent income and a good standard of living. I just could not accept that I was now earning money as a laborer.

Most Asian cultures, particularly the Chinese culture, value making a living by using one's brain over one's muscles. Moving boxes was a demeaning chore for me, and I was tremendously humbled. I felt I had reached the lowest point of my life. Late in the afternoon, when the sky was gray and a cold breeze was blowing in from a bay near the hotel, I thought of Dad and wondered how he would feel about his son making a living as a laborer. I looked down to hide the tears in my eyes.

Thankfully, more interesting assignments came along during the months that followed. I was involved in a special program of exchanging lockbox master keys for local real estate agents. I even made phone calls to constituents of a local politician and gave internal phone support for a local corporation. I began to find the assignments fascinating and to enjoy the variety.

In hindsight, those unique firsthand experiences gave me a broader perspective on work and confidence in my ability to support my family in ways I had never imagined. While the temporary jobs were overall a difficult experience, they taught me a big lesson: *The past is gone; live in the present and plan for the future* (see "The present is better than the past," page 97).

Though my financial struggle was truly painful, I found that my positive attitude was eradicating any short-lived moments of distress. I decided to regard the difference between the earnings I had expected and the little money I was actually earning as a *membership fee* I had to pay for the privilege of living in the United States. From that perspective, it was a bargain.

In San Diego alone, I had so many new adventures. During that period, I took over flying a single-engine plane for a few minutes with a pilot name Clarke Hewitt by my side. I fired an AK-47 at a shooting range, barbecued at parks by the bay and by the lake, watched fireworks at SeaWorld just across from my apartment, and attended many free concerts at San Diego Wild Animal Park (now San Diego Zoo Safari Park). I tried my hand at deep-sea fishing, sailing in the harbor, hot-air balloon rides, and horseback riding, and I enjoyed the sight of Fourth of July parades and fireworks. Such exciting activities and events were hard to come by in Hong Kong, and even if I could have accessed them, I would have had to pay a hefty price to attend.

Our friends Connie and Julius continued to offer us tremendous support during our hardship years. Not only did we become members of their extended family and attend many of their memorable family gatherings, but they also helped us increase our income. They introduced us to many of their relatives and friends, one of whom would later become my biggest insurance client. Julius enabled Teresa to contribute much-needed income to the family by hiring her to work at his restaurant.

But, When the Going Gets Tough, the Tough *Get to Know the Value of Money!*

Through my financial hardship, I developed a great deal of respect for the value of money (see "Money at work is better than you at work," page 101). The choice of spending or saving became simple. When deciding whether or not to buy something, I would ask myself if that item was worth the many hours I had to put in as a temporary worker to pay for it. I generally concluded that it was not. I would then look to see if there was a way I could live without it or if I already owned something similar. Did I need it or did I want it? That was when I began to recognize the significance of *less is more* (see "Simplicity is better than complexity," page 119).

A book that inspired me to live a frugal life was *Cashing in on the American Dream: How to Retire at 35*, by Paul Terhorst. Even though the book was published in 1984, most of the investment ideas and personal monetary management advice are still applicable today.[4] That book was my wake-up call. I adopted a frugal lifestyle and applied consistent discipline in managing my money. Mom was a splendid role model. How I wished I had picked up her traits when I was younger. With my new frugality, I slowly began to build a solid foundation for my future financial security.

Accumulation can be a very powerful force because of its subtle and latent strength. There are two types of accumulation powers: constructive and destructive. For example, saving money systematically is a constructive use of accumulation power; gradually gaining more debt is destructive (see "Money at work is better than you at work," on page 101). Constructive accumulation is helpful to our financial well-being; destructive accumulation is detrimental. An effortless way to achieve wealth creation is by avoiding destructive accumulation. During my years of financial struggle, I made a vow to never, ever carry any personal debt.

During the early 1980s, software for personal computers was readily available. I designed a spreadsheet using a computer software application to budget and record my monthly income and expenses. Having a budget gave me control of my money. Later, I switched the records over to Quicken, a personal finance software developed by Intuit. Never in my wildest dreams did I imagine that, 10 years later, I would be an employee of Intuit.

In time, I started sorting money into separate bank accounts named for specific purposes. Soon I expanded my thinking to a concept I came to call *reverse financing*—that is, instead of *buy now* and *pay later*, I would *pay now* (put money aside in a designated cash reserve account) and *buy later*. Part of the magic of this idea was that I received investment returns from the savings rather than paying interest to the debt, getting me to my target sooner. During my difficult financial period, despite the hardship, I managed to systematically save money for a down payment for our first condo. And to this day, I do not carry any personal debt.

But, When the Going Gets Tough, the Tough Go *Visiting Open Houses for Fun!*

One of the fun things Teresa and I did during the weekends was attend model home tours. We learned so much about floor plan designs, decor, and the market value of houses. Walking from one house to the next and climbing stairs to see the bedrooms was great physical exercise. We also got to know a lot about the communities we visited. Best of all, it was free. Some developers even served soft drinks and snacks. For many years, wherever we went, we always looked for open-house flags and signs.

The knowledge and experience we gained on these tours served me well when I was ready to buy my first condo. Though the mortgage loan process was complicated by my lack of employment history, I was eventually able to buy a two-story condo in Mission Valley in the heart of San Diego. I had always rented back in Hong Kong, so this condo was my very first experience of being a property owner. The pride of ownership gave me a powerful sense of freedom and satisfaction. I still recall the wonderful thrill and gratification I felt when I sat for the first time, with a glass of wine, on the patio of my own condo.

But, When the Going Gets Tough, the Tough Go *Running!*

During my hectic work weeks back in Hong Kong, I always looked forward to Sunday mornings, when I would jog along the trail of Victoria Peak on Hong Kong Island. In those early hours, I enjoyed a brief but invigorating time of quiet and serenity. The air was fresh and the view of the misty Hong

Kong harbor from 1,800 feet above was breathtaking. The city was busy and congested, and physical exercise, such as jogging, was an effective means for me to relieve the stress of urban living. I had always wanted to complete a marathon, but at that time I did not have the discipline or a suitable place for serious training. Running a marathon became one of my medium-term physical goals.

Completing a marathon is a remarkable goal partly because it is easily measurable (an important feature in a goal), but mostly because it is challenging enough to make it a major accomplishment while still being attainable. (Read more about the characteristics of a goal in Part Three.) For most participants, I believe the best part of running a marathon is the idea of *completing* rather than *competing*.

Now, with my flexible schedule, the fine weather, and the many open trails in San Diego, my past goal resurfaced. I was ready to start my training and fulfill my dream of completing a marathon.

I drew up a plan and started training along the concrete footpath around San Diego's beautiful Mission Bay. The location was ideal because it was fairly level and there were handy markings on the ground each quarter mile. This is where I met Jim, my neighbor, who was also running regularly around the bay.

Jim had completed many marathons (including the world-famous Boston Marathon), making him the perfect companion to motivate me. Whenever our paths crossed along the trail, he would cheer me on and give me lots of encouragement. Jim became my running buddy, and eventually he and his wife, Jennifer, became our best family friends.

Gradually, I increased my daily running distance. I took the long-and-short approach, alternating between long-distance and short-distance run days. Sunday was my super-long-distance run day. As part of my training agenda, I completed two 10Ks and one half-marathon before the marathon run.

Marathon training, I found, was more for the mind than for the body. I decided to run every day, regardless of how I felt. If my schedule was busy, I would run before the start of my work day in order not to miss the training. This marathon training taught me the importance of tenacity in completing any challenging long-term goal. The lessons learned would later help me successfully complete my master's thesis and doctoral dissertation.

A little over a year after I started training, and almost five years since I had become a resident of San Diego, I was ready. On December 12, 1988, at age 43, I ran the San Diego International Marathon. The weather was excellent for a long-distance run. The scenery around San Diego Harbor and Balboa Park was fabulous. I jogged along the designated route of 26 miles and 385 yards, one step at a time.

Six hours after the start time, marathon staff were starting to take apart the structures at the finish line. Teresa was ready to drive around to see if she could find me lying somewhere unconscious when there I was, a few blocks away, jogging slowly toward the finish line. I completed that marathon in 6 hours and 20 minutes. Later that day, I proudly brought my medal over to show Jim, my running-buddy neighbor. When he opened the door, he saw me standing there on a pair of wobbly legs with a big grin on my face.

But, When the Going Gets Tough, the Tough Get *U.S. Citizenship!*

Our five-year milestone as residents meant that our whole family was now eligible to apply for U.S. citizenship. To prepare for the interview, Teresa and I attended a citizenship preparation class. We then sent in our applications and eagerly awaited the big day. Teresa, Janette, and Mary-Ann were all born in Hong Kong and held British passports. I, on the other hand, was technically stateless. On my Hong Kong identity card, my nationality was marked as Eurasian. The connotation of this quasi-nationality was that I was a third-class citizen. It was quite depressing for me to watch my family going to a different immigration check-in line when we returned from a trip abroad.

I was born in an area of the old Shanghai French Concession in China.[5] Mom was Chinese and I was told that Dad was of Portuguese descent, though according to a recent DNA ancestry test I am 96.7 percent Asian. I did not have a birth certificate. The only document showing my date of birth was my baptismal certificate, which is in French. While I was a resident of Hong Kong, I was neither a British subject nor a Chinese citizen. Whenever I traveled, I had to use a Certificate of Identity booklet issued by the government of Hong Kong in lieu of a passport. This certificate did not give me protection by the British government when I was traveling outside of Hong Kong. I had to apply for a visa from any country I planned to visit.

My stateless status bothered me every time I had to fill in my nationality on a form. I felt odd when people asked me about my nationality or asked me to explain why I had a non-Chinese family name. Ethnic Chinese make up more than 90 percent of the population of Hong Kong.

That reminds me of the following tale:

Once upon a time, a bat flying toward a flock of birds asked whether it could join them.

The bat told the birds, "I am one of you because I can fly."

"No, you are not one of us," the birds said. "You don't have any feathers and you have four legs."

Feeling rejected, the bat crawled to a pack of rats and asked them, "Please let me join you because I have fur like you and I have four legs."

"No, you are not like us," the rats said to the bat. "You can fly, and we can't. Go away!"

Was I considered a bat? I had a non-Chinese family name, I was not recognized as a citizen by the British government, and I did not want to be associated with the Chinese communist government. The worst thing was that I was often made fun of and belittled by my peers and high school classmates for being a "mixed-breed" kid—a derogatory label only slightly better than "bastard." Today, mixed-blood is a more respectful label.

The pain of my stateless status was finally relieved on March 3, 1989, when I became a proud citizen of the United States. From my perspective, granting U.S. citizenship to a stateless person is akin to giving sight to a blind person. The naturalization ceremony took place at the War Memorial Building Auditorium near the San Diego Zoo. Mom; Thurman, Warren, Clarke, and their spouses; and a few members from the class I was teaching at that time attended to support us. It was a moving experience for my whole family. The hall was full of people, and we could feel an elevated level of energy inside. Together, my family took our oath of allegiance. I remember my mixed feelings of solemnity and excitement. The sweetest sound I heard that morning was the first three words in the congratulatory speech given by the judge after the oath: "My Fellow Americans . . ."

As soon as I walked out of the auditorium, I quickly registered to vote (a privilege I didn't have before). Our guests all gathered around and congratulated us with a lot of warm hugs and handshakes, and Clarke gave me my very own American flag!

When I walked outside the building, I looked up to the beautiful blue San Diego sky. I held my head high and felt like an eagle soaring.

"To heck with the birds and the rats. I don't need to join either of them after all!" I yelled out in my head. "I am now an American bald eagle and they are my prey!"

3. Accomplishing Years
1992 to 2002

Nothing builds self-esteem and
self-confidence like accomplishment.
—THOMAS CARLYLE

AN INSEPARABLE aspect of citizenship is taxation. The first time I tried to complete my tax return, I quickly found out that the tax system of the United States is complicated. One morning in 1984, I proudly told an American friend that I had successfully completed my very first U.S. tax return. To my surprise, he said, "What about California?" I was shocked. Hong Kong has a simple flat tax. The Hong Kong individual income tax form consisted of just two pages at that time and there was only one government, not two. How could tax systems be so complicated?

In spite of this complexity (or perhaps because of it), the U.S. tax form instructions aroused my curiosity. I had some knowledge of U.S. taxes prior to coming to America. Federal Income Taxation was part of the curriculum of the Chartered Life Underwriter (CLU) program I had completed when I was in Hong Kong.[6] As I had plenty of spare time during my early months, I began to study the tax form instructions line by line. They were fascinating. Completing the tax form seemed more like putting together a challenging puzzle.

For the uninitiated, here's a random example from the IRS instructions for Form 1040:

Combine the amounts from Form 1040, lines 7, 8a, 9a, 10 through 14, 15b, 16b, 17 through 19, and 21. Enter the amount, if any, from Form 1040, line 8b. Combine lines 2, 3, and 4. Enter the total of the amounts from Form 1040, lines 23 through 32, plus any write-in adjustments you entered on the dotted line next to line 36.[7]

One day, a year after I became a U.S. citizen, during my daily ritual of searching for other sources of income, I spotted an advertisement for an income tax course offered by H&R Block. That idea appealed to me, as I thought of myself as a meticulous person and I liked to work with numbers—a trait undoubtedly picked up from Dad. I signed up to take the class and quickly became even more fascinated by the complexity of individual income taxation in the United States. When I finished the course, I was offered a position as a seasonal/temporary tax preparer at one of the H&R Block branches near my condo.

At H&R Block, we had to complete tax returns in front of each client by the end of the first interview (unless the client was missing information). This was quite a daunting task. We entered the numbers on the tax forms by hand using a pencil and computed amounts using a desktop 10-key–style printing calculator.

After one December-to-April tax season at H&R Block, I was promoted to part-time office manager of a nearby branch. One of the unpleasant responsibilities of an office manager was handling demanding and difficult clients. The most frequent complaint was that we did not calculate an adequate tax refund. One client even asked me how much deduction was needed to get a specific amount of tax refund. (*Are you serious?*) Nobody likes to deal with the evils of taxation, which sometimes bring out our weakest side. Doing income taxes for the public taught me a lot about human behavior.

Teresa and I worked very hard. She clocked up many hours each day, seven days a week, at Julius's restaurant. I solicited and serviced insurance business during week days, instructed at Dale Carnegie classes on certain evenings, and pre- pared taxes at H&R Block on weekends and other evenings. Making ends meet required real effort—sometimes quite a lot. Financial success doesn't just happen.

A Career Breakthrough

Back in the 1970s, my youngest brother, Tom, gave me an Apple II desktop computer, which then cost nearly as much as a used car. This Apple II is what triggered my enthusiasm for personal computing. Later, I replaced it with an IBM PC. I taught myself the programming language of BASIC and learned to create spreadsheets using VisiCalc and to build databases using DB2. Personal computers were just starting to enter the consumer market. I had no idea that this technology would eventually bestow upon me a full-time career in a far- off country.

Fast-forward to the summer of 1992, when I was still work- ing part-time at H&R Block. A colleague mentioned to me that there were openings for seasonal testers for a tax-preparation software development company, and that it was paying almost three times what I was making. The company was looking for people with a tax background, enough knowledge to use a personal computer, and a willingness to work for just a few months. Those requirements fit both of us perfectly. Eager for a fresh start, I was extremely interested in getting this job. Together, my colleague and I went for our interviews—and were hired instantly. The company was ChipSoft, the maker of TurboTax.[8] Tax-preparation software was rapidly becoming a trendy way for Americans to prepare their tax returns.

That fall day in 1992 when I first reported for work at ChipSoft was a major turning point in my life in the United States. It marked the beginning of my accomplishing years. My supervisor assigned me a desk inside a room, where I sat alone among several bookcases lined with tax code manuals from the Internal Revenue Service and tax agencies of various state governments. This was probably the perfect spot for me, as I had always loved books and I would later come to think of one particular library as my second home. On the outside of the door was a plate with my name, below which was another plate that said "Library." One day, a senior programmer was passing by the door. "Hey . . . you are so lucky!" he said. "A library is named after you and you didn't even have to die!"

It didn't take long for me to see how busy things could get at a growing tax software development company. In November, the busiest month of that first year, I clocked up 16 hours a day for a consecutive 13 days. I was the QA (Quality Assurance) Lead, and I needed to be on duty until everything was signed off and ready to be delivered to Customer Acceptance. It might have been grueling, but I certainly wasn't complaining: I was getting double time for hours worked beyond 12. I got several handsome paychecks!

The success of TurboTax led to a rapid expansion of the company. After one year as a seasonal/temporary employee, I was offered a full-time position as a Tax Analyst Programmer. After living in the United States for close to 10 years, I finally had a full-time job. My assignments included analyzing and coding the instructions of federal individual income tax forms. Things started happening fast, and soon ChipSoft was bought by the publicly traded financial software giant Intuit.

The early 1990s saw an historic and mind-blowingly rapid development of information technology and the exponential growth of a new thing called the Internet. Working in a high-tech company, I was lucky to see many innovative technological advancements. The earlier applications of TurboTax were developed using Apple Macintosh computers running Mac OS and later ones used personal computers (PCs) running Microsoft Windows, so I became proficient with both operating systems. The knowledge and experience I was gaining would greatly enhance my teaching later in my academic career. For instance, if I was giving lectures on topics related to PC history, I could share many real-world events from my experience at Intuit.

During my years at Intuit, I was given many opportunities to learn computer programming languages, form-design tools, and software quality testing techniques, and about income taxation. Through the support and encouragement of Intuit's leadership and generous financial incentive, I completed a series of intensive tax courses and passed the difficult Enrolled Agent exam, qualifying me to represent taxpayers before the IRS. Later in my career, I coded various parts of the software, including electronic filing, when that alternative to paper filing was in its infancy.

In one of the Tax Development team meetings at Intuit, I flashed back to the dilemma of being a "bat," not accepted by either the birds or the rats. I told everyone in the meeting that we should remind other teams within the organization of our skill set and qualifications relating to our job title. The programming teams addressed us as TAs (Tax Analysts), not recognizing us as programmers, although we also wrote some fairly complex code. And our QA teams addressed us as programmers, not considering us qualified tax professionals, although most of us were experienced tax preparers, EAs, or CPAs. I said emphatically, "For goodness' sake, we are all TAPs (Tax Analyst Programmers). We are knowledgeable about both computer programming and income taxation, and we are proud of our job title as TAPs!"

This reminds me of a statement I made during another team meeting. As part of our job, we had to count and verify the number of characters in the input fields of the forms we designed. I boldly proclaimed, "As TAPs, we don't just count characters, but character *counts!*"

The tax software program we developed was an example of a built-in expert system. It included a database of tax knowledge that, in addition to calculating a user's taxes, could offer advice and guidance based on the user's specific tax data input. Honestly, I felt privileged to be associated with the talented team of experts in my department and, over the years, to work under several outstanding project managers. Those great leaders gave me generous support and encouragement to do my job well.

Capping off this support was the opportunity to fulfill my desire to pursue higher education. Mavash Atoufi, my manager, came into my office one day and told me that the company had just approved a generous employee tuition aid program and asked if I was interested. Her three soft knocks on my door turned out to be a pivotal moment in my life.

Finally Going to College at Age 53

In 1998, I seized the tuition aid offered by Intuit and began my full-time study toward an undergraduate degree. I had to start my work day at the office at 7:30 a.m. so I could leave early to attend classes starting at 6:00 p.m. Despite the sacrifices, I thoroughly enjoyed being a full-time student again. I studied many humanities and social science subjects I had never been exposed to before, including sociology, psychology, and critical thinking.

During my first college year, I felt somewhat degraded when I was required to take algebra—a subject I had aced in high school 35 years before (college-level algebra was a part of the curriculum during the final year of high school in Hong Kong). The algebra was a prerequisite and, sadly, I had no transfer of equivalent credit that was recognized by my university. That was also the reason I had to take a lot of courses in general education. Nonetheless, having a strong background in algebra did give me a good foundation for learning programming languages, because the logic learned in algebra could be useful in defining programming algorithms.

The two and a half years I spent completing my BS degree in Information Systems were exceptionally accomplishing years. I gained more knowledge during that time than in all the many years of higher education that I later pursued. The completion of my undergraduate degree fulfilled my long-term educational goal. If granting citizenship to a stateless person was like giving sight to a blind person, getting a college degree at a mature age was like regaining mobility after being paralyzed.

I was the second college graduate among three generations of the Cruz family. My youngest daughter, Mary-Ann, beat me by one year. We were both first-generation college students.

Mom and Dad had no college education, so Mom was very proud. I know Dad would have been, too.

On the day of my graduation, Mom did not know I was about to participate in my commencement ceremony. I told her we were going to have lunch at a restaurant in downtown San Diego with Connie and Julius, together with Betty and Raymond, who had come down from Los Angeles. At the end of lunch, I quickly sneaked to the restroom and put on my cap and gown. I walked out and proudly told Mom that we were all going to my graduation ceremony.

The commencement was held at San Diego Convention Center inside the Sails Pavilion on a beautiful sunny afternoon in May 2000. Lines of faculty and graduates marched slowly into the hall with thousands of friends and family members cheering. I thought I was walking on air as I marched to the background music of *Pomp and Circumstance March #1* during the procession of my first commencement. Even after many years, whenever I hear this famous piece, commonly known as the graduation march, it still sends chills through me. Mom was elated because her son was finally graduating from college. Walking across the graduation stage, I said softly to myself, "Mom, I made it!"

Afterwards, we had a party at my house, where many friends and relatives gathered to congratulate me. At age 55, I finally got to celebrate my very first college graduation. One of my friends sent me a note joking about the worthlessness of a degree for a person my age. To me, my age was not important; it was the accomplishment of one of my long-term goals that mattered. As the saying goes, "Age is just a number."

During the graduation party, there was no doubt in my mind. . . .

The *Study* Must Go On!

Graduation is referred to as "commencement" because it symbolizes both the end of one cycle and the beginning of another. I took this literally. After I completed my undergraduate degree, I went straight to graduate school.

When I was completing my undergraduate degree, I found the subject of psychology very interesting. That was my first choice for a graduate program. However, it was unlikely that my company would subsidize the tuition for a field of study not directly related to my job. Instead, though the thought of getting a graduate degree in psychology stayed with me, I chose to pursue a Master of Business Administration (MBA) degree with a specialization in Technology Management.

A Financial Breakthrough

While achieving my mental (intellectual) goal of pursuing my college degree, I was also achieving the financial goal of investing in my first residential rental property. The accumulation of funds from the generous stock options offered by Intuit, the regular inflow of dividends from my Hong Kong company, and my disciplined savings habit began to build up quickly. I was ready to explore investment opportunities.

In my goal-setting method, I establish short-, medium-, and long-term goals (see Part Three for more about goal setting). My medium-term financial goal since coming to the U.S. had been to invest in real estate. During the early 1990s, when getting a mortgage was relatively easy and the required down payment was low, I began to look for residential rental properties. Through a Realtor friend, I bought my first residential rental property. Later, I gradually bought several more using the money I saved and the income received from the properties I owned. This was the period when I came to recognize that *money at work is better than you at work* (see page 101) and the crucial importance of location in real estate investment.

In general, I think carrying debt is "bad." However, having a mortgage, a student loan, or an auto loan may be "good." Very few people can buy a house with cash, but everyone needs to have a home to live in. A student loan is good because higher levels of education do result in a higher income. Getting an auto loan could be a smart move if you need to commute to work. The return on investment from those "good" loans (in most cases) far exceeds the interest paid.

I once read that *those who understand interest earn it; those who don't, pay it!* For this reason, I always pay off my credit card balance in full every month. I also have a system that regularly puts money aside as a reserve for any major purchases, such as a new car (see reverse financing, page 109). I have never had a car loan because all my automobiles (eight in the last 30-plus years) were bought with cash.

I have always been interested in investing in equity. I adopted the buy-and-hold strategy because I came to believe that *one can't time the market.* It is time in the market that builds returns, not market timing. Equity investment is another good example of *money at work.*

A medium-term financial goal on my list since I had begun earning money was to attend investment conferences and seminars for learning and inspiration. Over the years, I have had the honor of meeting Charles Schwab, as well as David and Tom Gardner of the popular investment website The Motley Fool.[9]

Through owning one special stock, I had the privilege of attending a spectacular and memorable shareholders' meeting in Omaha, Nebraska. I was fortunate to meet and have my photograph taken with Warren Buffett, the chairman of Berkshire Hathaway. Known as the Oracle of Omaha, Mr. Buffet is the investment guru of our times, and one of the richest and most respected businessmen in the world.[10]

The fun part of attending the Berkshire Hathaway's annual meeting of shareholders was to visit the trade show booths with products and services from its own companies. The official meeting started with a video showing Mr. Buffett playing the ukulele and singing. The formal business was short and efficient. The *ayes* on seconding the motions were unanimous. After the formality of motions and votes, the board of directors responded to questions from the shareholders.

I could feel the spirit of gigantic wealth inside the auditorium. I looked at the people around me and reminded myself that my net worth must be among the lowest of the attendees. *But it was so much better to be among the bottom in a wealthier group than among the top in a less wealthy group* (see page 77). When I was at the bottom, I could look up and be inspired by successful role models.

My First Step into Single-Family Home Ownership

In 1992, the purchase of my very first single-family house as my own residence in the United States meant another important turnaround in my life. I felt I could finally stand up on my own and take my first step. In fact, after I moved to the single-family house in Poway, I named it *The First Step*. (I named the next house I bought, at Rancho Bernardo, *The Second Step*.)

Through my real estate agent, I bought this first house from the Resolution Trust Corporation. It was a foreclosed property, and the Savings and Loan Association that took it over soon also filed for bankruptcy. As a result, the property was sold *as is* at an attractive price. My research into real estate had taught me the importance of due diligence. Before I made my final offer, I hired a building inspector to evaluate the condition of the property. Based on the report, I calculated the added costs of a few minor repairs and negotiated a lower selling price. That house turned out to be a very good investment, with the property value appreciating threefold over the next 10 years.

I still have special memories of living in The First Step. The house was somewhat hidden because it was slightly below street level, on a large wooded lot near a creek that was dry during most of the year. There were plenty of flower bushes, mature trees, and a few tall fruit trees. The back garden was often visited by hawks, blue jays, raccoons, skunks, coyotes, and even a peacock once! Living in a 2,500-square-foot single-family house with a detached garage on over an *acre* of land was a tremendous change indeed from living in an 800-square-foot apartment.

Lessons learned: *location, location, and location.* When choosing between two houses of comparable prices, it is much better to buy the one in a good neighborhood. While I was deciding on any purchase, I would drive around the area both during the day and at night. I would check the people out in the nearby grocery stores, retailers, and businesses. Also, I understood it is very important to include the ease of later selling the house in my final decision. Due diligence, I learned, is imperative.

But, When the Going Gets Accomplishing, the Accomplished Go *Free!*

Having a great house, a few residential rental properties, and a portfolio of stocks, I thought perhaps the time was right for me to contemplate the "R" word. The true meaning of retirement for me was the opportunity, freedom, and resources to do whatever I wanted. I believed I had achieved my financial independence and I was ready to look for something I wanted to do without any time and budget constraints. I still had quite a few items on my bucket list (though I prefer the more positive phrase wish list). I also realized I needed to start paying attention to my long-term goals while I was still relatively young and healthy. I had come to believe that anyone can retire at any time if they are willing to align their level of living standards with their available resources (see "Half-full is better than half-empty," on page 85).

In the summer of 2002, at the age of 57, I retired from the position of Tax Analyst Programmer at Intuit with my freshly achieved financial freedom and the confidence it gave me. The farewell party was fun and heartwarming. My colleagues showered me with high-tech gifts because I had mentioned to one of them that I was interested in artificial intelligence.

Still, in the first few months after I left my job, I felt uneasy when people asked me what I did for a living. I had been associating too much of my identity with my job title. Without it, I felt lost, and I was not ready to admit I was retired. If freedom was what I was striving for, I needed to disconnect my profession from my personal identity.

It took me a while to accept that I am who I am, not what I do.

Play is generally defined as an activity engaged in for enjoyment and recreation, while work has the primary goal of producing income. When one enjoys working at something without thinking too much about earning an income, that work can become play! I have always enjoyed going back to full-time study for this very reason: to me it feels more like play than work.

A Student Speaker at My Graduation Commencement

An event that made me feel very proud was my second graduation commencement, this time for my MBA. Like my first, it was held at the San Diego Convention Center. But this time, I was honored to be selected from over 100 candidates as a student speaker to address the graduating class! What a wonderful once-in-a-lifetime graduation gift for me!

On that special day, I proudly walked among the Dean and faculty members at the beginning of the procession (with that wonderfully familiar graduation march playing in the background). Mom was even happier this time as she watched her son march across the hall and up to the platform.

It was quite a magnificent view looking down from the podium at thousands of graduates, families, and friends below. I could see a sea of black caps in front of me (some, I remember, were decorated with flashy designs).

I looked at the crowd and paused for a second. As soon as I announced, "My fellow graduates . . . Class of 2002 . . . Congratulations . . ." roaring cheers of thousands of attendees echoed inside the hall!

4. Freedom Years
2003 to Present

Man is free at the moment he wishes to be.
—VOLTAIRE

TEACHING HAD ALWAYS been play rather than work to me. I was ready to follow my passion for teaching—because, really, I couldn't think of anything else I would rather do. The timing was right for me to pursue more graduate education while looking for a career in academia.

A Full-Time Faculty Career

Never underestimate the power of connections or meeting the right person at the right time. Back when I first arrived in the U.S., I was able to reconnect with the Dale Carnegie Institute at San Diego through my past instructors in Hong Kong. And now, in 2002, through Sameh El Naggar, a classmate in my MBA program, I met with John Bugado, the department chair of Computer Science and Information Systems at National University.

I later learned about a further connection: it turned out that John was the husband of Claire, the manager of the H&R Block office where I had worked one tax season when I wanted to get hands-on knowledge of the new tax-preparation software. Claire's endorsement might have added some weight to the final acceptance of my adjunct faculty application. Anyway, thanks in part to my connections, I was hired. After about a year of retirement, I was back in the workforce.

John was always a wonderful and supportive department chair. He helped me get started in a field that was new to me. I couldn't have found a better person to guide me through my transition into a career in academia. As a bonus, John and I became good friends.

The first course I taught was Internet Marketing. Information technology related to this subject was emerging at that time, and I had to keep up to date with the rapid and ongoing development of the Internet, electronic-commerce, and electronic-logistics. Later, I would teach courses on information technology management, information systems, and business knowledge management. From my research and preparation, I gained a great deal of knowledge about the subjects I taught. Teaching is indeed the best way to learn.

I jumped from the rank of adjunct to certified core adjunct, then to a half-time position of associate faculty. After two years, I became the lead faculty of the Bachelor of Science in Information Systems program. During those years, I acquired a working knowledge of curriculum design and of program and course learning outcome design and mapping, and I took part in several school- and university-level committees. I also served in the university senate, a governing body made up of members of the faculty in university planning and governance.

One of my happiest days in academia was the day I was offered a full-time position as an instructor—the lowest rank of a full-time faculty. As a full-time employee, I was getting a handsome package of employee benefits, including medical insurance (which had been costing me handsomely each month since leaving Intuit). I had finally achieved my goal of a career in a higher-education institution and attained one of my medium-term external financial (career) goals (see the goal-planning matrix example on page 177). After my brief retirement, I was back to full-time work with a brand-new job title in which to frame my identity. I was back to *I am what I do.*

I felt privileged to be associated with a team of such highly educated scholars. One day, soon after I became a full-time faculty, I attended our regular school meeting. I was sitting in the back row watching professors entering the room a few at a time. They all greeted each other as "Doctor." (*Am I in a hospital?*) I felt truly humbled to be among them. I flashed back to attending the shareholders meeting of Berkshire Hathaway. Once again, I could feel the spirit of profound knowledge inside a room. I looked at the scholars around me and reminded myself that in this room I was the person with the lowest educational qualification. *But it was so much better to be among the bottom in a highly educated group than among the top in a less educated group* (see page 77). At the bottom in a better group, I was more likely to look up and be inspired by the successful role models surrounding me.

An added benefit of being a full-time faculty was the opportunity to attend academic conferences all over the world. I attended and presented scholarly papers at conferences in many cities in the United States, Canada, South Korea, the United Kingdom—and even Hong Kong.

I thoroughly enjoyed my time in the classroom teaching and helping students. Most of my students were working adults who were highly motivated to complete their degrees. They brought with them many valuable experiences related to the subjects I was teaching. Sometimes I thought I was more of a student than an instructor. This time, instead of *paying* to learn, I was *paid* to learn. What a deal!

One late afternoon, I was teaching a class on National University's campus at the Naval Amphibious Base Coronado right across the bay from downtown San Diego. During the break, I was standing outside to enjoy the fresh sea breeze when a team of Navy SEALs walked by in full white uniform. They had just come from their graduation ceremony and were cheering and talking happily with each other. I was totally stunned by the sight of such an elite team of individuals leisurely filing pass me. At that moment, I reaffirmed—with moist eyes—that I was so proud to be an American citizen. I was also extremely lucky to be in the right place at the right time. Not too many people have a chance to see and feel the vibrancy of such a magnificent group of individuals up close.

The *Study* Keeps Going!

The academic environment stimulated me to go further in my studies, and I earned two more advanced degrees while I was actively teaching.

Almost as soon as I had completed my MBA, I pursued a second master's degree in human behavior. I realized I should keep up my education while my quest for knowledge was still driven by the momentum and habit of studying.

Ever since my work preparing tax returns and programming tax software, I had been fascinated by the unorthodox behavior of individuals and the social behavior of people in groups. The tax program was designed to intelligently interact with users, but some of those users behaved in ways I found surprising. I wanted to find out more about why people behave the way they do.

I was fascinated to learn how behavior is typically affected and shaped by tradition, culture, religion, and the charisma of perceived leaders. I found the subject matter to be surprisingly far-reaching and complicated. It took me two years to complete my master's degree in human behavior, and in the end, I honestly believed I had just scratched the surface of this topic.[11]

Most higher education institutions require their professors to have earned a doctoral degree in their field. As I had the time and the resources to pursue a terminal degree, I did not hesitate to take on a new challenge. The decision as to what area I would research was easy. I chose knowledge management, a subarea of information systems that covers a broad range of underlying disciplines. They include epistemology, information technology, learning management, expert systems, and decision support systems, as well as research in decision sciences. I was having fun going back to full-time study again.

I started to research the definitions of information and knowledge and the connections between them. I quickly found that knowledge is an important business asset. An organization's ability to keep and use its business knowledge is fundamental to gaining a strong competitive advantage. Its business knowledge consists of the experience of its workforce, the know-how of its processes, and the understanding of the needs and wants of its customers. Yet, most organizations were not managing their knowledge well. Information is simply a collection of processed facts; it can generally be classified and retrieved with relative ease. But knowledge is the deeper understanding acquired through experience and education; it is more abstract and, naturally, more difficult to codify and maintain. Somehow, I was drawn to this subject.

While I was studying knowledge management, I found myself constantly applying the concepts of corporate knowledge to individual knowledge. Being educated is being knowledgeable. Knowledge, something nobody can take away, is truly an asset. Like a well-managed business, an educated person holds a competitive edge. Thus, there are huge advantages to being a lifelong learner. Setting mental goals (including practical knowledge and education) is as important to the well-being of an individual as setting health, financial, and social goals. (See more about balanced goals in Part Three.)

During the four years of my doctoral studies, I had the opportunity to attend residencies at the University of Minnesota in the United States and the University of Liverpool in the United Kingdom. Each time, I stayed in the dormitories and thoroughly enjoyed a few days' taste of campus life. Best of all, I had a chance to explore places with diverse cultures and get acquainted with fellow classmates and faculty from a multitude of backgrounds. It was truly an awesome learning experience. The journey was indeed greater than the destination.

At a time when I felt lost and alone, I had yet another experience of meeting the right person at the right time. A colleague introduced me to Dr. Sukie Stone, a doctoral degree mentor. I met Dr. Stone in the library where I was working hard on my research. Fulfilling the requirements of a dissertation is a complicated process, and Dr. Stone helped me untangle it. She gave me a lot of support and encouragement. In some ways, she reminded me of my marathon running buddy, Jim. Working on a doctoral dissertation was a lonely task, but Dr. Stone's kindness and guidance made me feel I was not alone on this long journey.

My dissertation was a case study analyzing views on knowledge sharing and the competitiveness of professional services firms. Through Dr. Stone, I met with an officer of a well-known international management consulting firm, where I was given permission to conduct in-depth interviews with its knowledge workers.

Completing my doctoral degree gave me another chance to use the tactics that had worked so well for me in my marathon training. I worked on my dissertation daily, regardless of how busy I was.[12] By spending most of my non-teaching time at the university library, I successfully completed and defended my dissertation in less than two years. Once again, the completion of my doctoral degree meant the successful attainment of a significant long-term mental (education) goal.

A Doctoral Degree at Age 66

During one of my several trips back to Hong Kong, I revisited the university that had rejected me 50 years earlier. I walked proudly through the main entrance—with a bachelor's degree, two master's degrees, a doctoral degree, and a sly smile on my face.

In a letter Dad wrote me nearly 40 years ago, he told me:

I admire you for your thirst for education . . . I had less than five years' schooling. Earning a living during the 1930s and 40s was much easier. Nowadays, the business is so advanced and complex trying to secure employment without a college degree will be difficult . . .

Had he still been with us, I wonder what Dad would have said to me on the day of my doctoral commencement.

In the summer of 2011, I attended my fourth commencement, this time for my PhD, in Minneapolis, Minnesota. The ceremony took place in the Minneapolis Convention Center. We were honored to have President Bill Clinton as our keynote speaker. As he walked in, we all stood up and gave him a roaring ovation. The way he looked at the audience, his gestures, and his skillful use of pauses showed that he was truly a superb speaker. He delivered a strong message to encourage all the graduates to accept the responsibility of creating positive change for humanity.[13]

In my doctoral cap and gown, I walked proudly into the hall with a live band playing the graduation march. Somehow it sounded even better this time. It was an emotional moment for me when I walked up the steps to the stage for my hooding ceremony and heard my name announced as "Dr. Albert Patrick Cruz."

It seemed to me that President Clinton's Secret Service agents were keeping an eye on William Wong, my brother-in-law from Toronto, as he sneaked closer and closer to the stage to take pictures. The ceremony was broadcast live over the Internet, and I knew a lot of my friends and family were watching.

Sixty years had passed between my graduating from kindergarten and attaining my doctoral degree. On a wall in my study hang my kindergarten and doctoral diplomas. Though just a few inches apart, they represent a span of six decades.

Back to Retirement Again

In 2012, after working full-time as a faculty at National University for several years, I decided to wind down a bit and move forward with my other goals. I left my full-time job to teach part-time as an adjunct. I preferred to devote my time to teaching rather than to administrative and program-management tasks. And with the extra time that gave me, I could enjoy reading books, listening to relaxing music in my dream sound room, taking photographic portraits of friends, and traveling to new cities and other places.

Since leaving my full-time teaching job, I have made numerous trips to San Francisco, Las Vegas, and Phoenix. I went to see the Winchester Mystery House and Computer History Museum in San Jose, and the Musical Instrument Museum in Phoenix. On one journey, I made a special drive from Phoenix to Casa Grande to visit Albert Cruz Park.[14] Yes, a park is named after me, and I didn't have to pay for it! (It's actually named after someone else with the same name.)

In cities nearby, I visited Carlsbad's Flower Field, Mission Inn's Festival of Lights, wineries in Temecula Valley, the Getty Center and Villa, and the Nixon Presidential Library. I also had a very special tour and lunch in the exclusive Club 33 inside Disneyland.[15] In short, I continue to enjoy the wonderful privilege of living in the United States.

Thanks to my freedom, I have been back to Hong Kong several times. During one of my visits, I stopped over in Tokyo. I stayed at the same hotel where, three decades earlier, I had called Dad just 10 days before he passed.[16] On a recent trip back to Hong Kong, I was invited to a 40th-anniversary reunion of one of my earlier Dale Carnegie classes.

As I get older, I am following the advice that happiness is spending money on experiences, not material things. Things come and go, but fond memories linger. I continue to both cross off and add items to my wish list (oh yes, skydiving and learning to play piano are still there).

But my interest in teaching has held strong. So, when opportunity knocked again, in 2013, not too long after my second retirement, I accepted an offer of a part-time faculty position from San Diego Mesa College.[17] It was great to be back in academia again.

The first day I stepped onto the campus of San Diego Mesa College as a faculty was quite emotional. The sky was blue, and

I was surrounded by several school buildings and the library (called the Learning Resource Center). Students were scattered all over the campus, some chatting on benches, others lying on the grass in the shade, reading. Up until now, I had associated only with non-traditional universities that lacked a central campus. It had taken me over half a century to journey from being rejected as a student by a university to becoming an adjunct professor at this traditional college.

Times had changed since the old days of college, and I now found myself teaching mostly online courses. The benefit of teaching online is that there is no need to commute. I could live anywhere. Teresa and I, now in our late sixties, decided it was time to settle down in a quieter and more relaxing location.

At the end of my first semester at San Diego Mesa College, we considered moving to somewhere between Los Angeles and San Diego. We made a few house-hunting trips from north of San Diego to east of Los Angeles. Finally, we found a city in Riverside County that is conveniently situated between the two metropolitan areas.

With the help of a real estate agent, we visited a few communities and finally found an ideal new housing development within a brand-new community. After we had chosen our lot, construction began. We drove by almost every week to watch the house being built. It was so much fun watching the building process. After about seven months, we moved in.

Around our new home, the air is fresh and the neighborhood is peaceful, with natural, tranquil surroundings. In order to maintain one of my short-term physical goals, I have been walking and jogging three miles around the nearby playground and neighboring streets every morning, accompanied by the sound of chirping birds. What a delightful way to start each day. The residence is away from the hustle and bustle of big cities, yet both Los Angeles and San Diego are just an hour's drive away. I named this home *The Desert Cottage*. Enough with the *Step* word I used for my first and second single-family homes. This house is a cozy hideaway for us to relax in and enjoy! I wrote this book there.

But not only there. The word *library* shows up here again, as I also spent quite a lot of time writing this book in the library of Mount San Jacinto College near my house.[18] Writing a book was one of my medium-term mental goals to be achieved after completing my doctoral degree.

Pursuit of Happiness

We may not have much control over extending our life, but we can certainly widen it by enjoying every moment and living life to the fullest. I continue to set new balanced goals, refine them, and achieve them, all while enjoying *the happiness of pursuit* throughout the process.[19]

San Diego International Airport,
December 1983

At Thurman's house on the second
day after our arrival in San Diego

Montgomery Field, San Diego

Escondido Police
Department Firing Range

Ramona Oaks Park, San
Diego Country Estates

A new U.S. citizen
registering to vote

Mission Bay, San Diego

San Diego International Marathon

QA at Intuit

Mr. Warren Buffet at
Berkshire Hathaway's AGM

Commencement speech,
San Diego Convention Center

First day teaching at
National University

THIS IS YOUR LIFE.

DO WHAT YOU LOVE,
AND DO IT OFTEN.

IF YOU DON'T LIKE SOMETHING, CHANGE IT.

IF YOU DON'T LIKE YOUR JOB, QUIT.

IF YOU DON'T HAVE ENOUGH TIME, STOP WATCHING TV.
IF YOU ARE LOOKING FOR THE LOVE OF YOUR LIFE, STOP;
THEY WILL BE WAITING FOR YOU WHEN YOU

START DOING THINGS YOU LOVE.

STOP OVER ANALYZING, ALL EMOTIONS ARE BEAUTIFUL.

LIFE IS SIMPLE.

WHEN YOU EAT, APPRECIATE
EVERY LAST BITE.

OPEN YOUR MIND, ARMS, AND HEART TO NEW THINGS
AND PEOPLE, WE ARE UNITED IN OUR DIFFERENCES.
ASK THE NEXT PERSON YOU SEE WHAT THEIR PASSION IS,
AND SHARE YOUR INSPIRING DREAM WITH THEM.

TRAVEL OFTEN;

GETTING LOST WILL
HELP YOU FIND YOURSELF.

SOME OPPORTUNITIES ONLY COME ONCE, SEIZE THEM.
LIFE IS ABOUT THE PEOPLE YOU MEET, AND
THE THINGS YOU CREATE WITH THEM
SO GO OUT AND START CREATING.

LIFE IS SHORT.

LIVE YOUR DREAM
AND SHARE
YOUR PASSION.

THE HOLSTEE MANIFESTO © 2009   HOLSTEE.COM   DESIGN BY RACHAEL BERESH

Manifesto courtesy of Holstee.

Visit holstee.com to learn more.

Part Two

NINE SIMPLE GUIDELINES
FOR AN ENRICHED LIFE

Introduction

FROM MY EARLY TWENTIES into my late thirties, my self-esteem was low. Young and naïve, I lacked willpower and self-discipline. I was overweight, lived beyond my means, and had a dim outlook on my life. You may recall that I experienced two emotionally disturbing incidents during my late teens and early twenties. Recollection of these continuously bothered me for over a decade, damaging my self-image and causing me to feel confused and mentally defeated.

During those miserable years, I had many questions about how to live, and I sought out answers with increasing vigor. As a keen reader and insatiable learner, I visited a library or a bookstore whenever I had the chance. Reading took my mind off my negative feelings and satisfied my curiosity with new knowledge. I immersed myself in my favorite subjects: self-help, health and fitness, personal finance, investing, and management science. As I read, I would jot down notes and formulate what would later become my guidelines to live by.

Among my favorite authors were Napoleon Hill (*Think and Grow Rich*), Earl Nightingale (*The Strangest Secret*), Denis Waitley (*The Psychology of Winning*), and Zig Ziglar (*See You at the Top*). I had the privilege of attending a presentation by Norman Vincent Peale, the author of *The Power of Positive Thinking*, when he visited Hong Kong during the mid-1970s.

In response to the inspiring messages in these books, I began to transform my attitude, gradually becoming a more positive and self-disciplined person. I started to get up at

6:00 a.m. (nowadays, I start my day at 4:00 a.m.!), take diligent care of my health, and systematically manage my finances.

In the field of management science, I found myself drawn to organization and method (O&M), now generally known as operations management or, with the adoption of current information technology, business analytics. From O&M techniques, I learned to become an organized person who keenly values efficiency. It is also thanks to O&M that my colleagues at all the places I have worked over the years would remark on the neatness (or emptiness) of my desk and work space.

In addition to reading, I was also enrolling in many evening and weekend classes to enhance my general and professional knowledge. While this may have been overcompensation for not getting into college immediately after high school, it really paid off.

The Dale Carnegie Turning Point

One of the self-help books I came across was *How to Win Friends and Influence People* by Dale Carnegie.[20] The book's messages were so eye-opening that, when the world-famous Dale Carnegie course was first offered in Hong Kong in 1975, I enrolled immediately. Attending the course was not only a crucial turning point for me in my late thirties, it also started my 15-year relationship with Dale Carnegie Training. The messages from Dale Carnegie helped me recognize that I had the ability to improve myself. I saw that it was up to me to change my future. I steadily regained my self-confidence. From then on, I was not afraid to take risks.

How I Developed the Guidelines

During the three-month Dale Carnegie course, I was highly motivated by class activities and the interactions among class members. The candid way my fellow class members shared their feelings through their talks moved me greatly. Shortly after the course ended, I took back control of my life, stepping up the efforts I had begun a few years earlier to improve my health, finances, knowledge, and relationships with others. As part of this vigorous new push in self-improvement, I started what would become a lifelong project of developing and fine-tuning my *guidelines for an enriched life and balanced goal setting.*

To help me stay motivated, I began to compile and organize the notes I had started to take when I first began reading inspirational books. Over the years, I would continue to organize and tag these notes, along with the goals I set myself, in a three-ring binder. With the emergence of computer software, I started entering the notes and goals digitally by using the spreadsheet program IBM Lotus 1-2-3 to make updating easier. Later, I switched to Microsoft Excel.

Most of the guidelines are based on my reading. Others came to me while I was listening to over a thousand talks given by the class members of the Dale Carnegie courses I taught in Hong Kong and the United States. A few were inspired by life's events and challenges. Over time, I often revised and enhanced the guidelines as I read and learned more—or, shall I say, as I learned from my mistakes.

I eventually decided on nine key guidelines. To name them, I chose a "compare and assess" construct (that is, "this approach is better than *that* approach, and here is why"), as I felt this gave a snapshot of each guideline's meaning.

For over four decades now, I have been following the *guidelines* and successfully achieving my balanced goals. They play an instrumental role when I have to make important decisions or resolve crucial issues. The guidelines give me a clear direction in which to look for alternatives. Oftentimes, they also serve as effective stress relievers, giving me the sense that a particular situation is under control.

The yin-yang philosophy illustrates the opposite but complementary forces of dark and light. Life is full of ups and downs, good and bad, positive and negative. Each of my guidelines focuses on the positive and ignores the negative. When we spend our energy and thoughts mostly on the positive, the negative will wither due to malnutrition. How nice!

Yin-Yang Symbol

Nine Simple Guidelines

FIVE OF MY NINE guidelines offer rationales for why we should take a positive approach, especially when confronted with conflict. The remaining four propose using common sense as a course of action and recommend looking at things from diverging perspectives. Even though more guidelines have evolved over the years, I consider these nine the most helpful and essential. Note that they are *not* listed in order of importance, as their relative importance will be different for everyone, and that importance may change according to circumstances.

- **Bottom in the best is better than top in the average.**
  We are better off among the best, even if we are near the bottom of the group. Among the best are plenty of good role models to look up to; being at the bottom gives us more room to grow.

- **Half-full is better than half-empty.**
  Half a glass of water has only one level. What matters is how we interpret that level. We are unhappy when we constantly chase what we lack. As soon as one desire is satisfied, a new one will show up almost instantly.

- **Walking toward is better than walking away.**

  It's natural to think that if we walk away from a problem, it will disappear. However, most often a problem can be effectively resolved if we confront it with the right attitude and constructive action.

- **The present is better than the past.**

  We can never turn back the pages of time and change what we have done. The past has passed. But we do have control of the present, which is why it should command our attention.

- **Money at work is better than you at work.**

  Isn't it great when we have extra helpers—in the form of interest, dividends, and capital gains—to produce income for us? The more fortune servants we recruit, the easier it is for us to build our wealth.

- **Responding is better than reacting.**

  To be responsive is to lessen the impact of a situation and give ourselves more time to evaluate. To react is to limit our options and give away control to others.

- **Simplicity is better than complexity.**

  When you're faced with complicated situations, break down the tasks and remove the "window dressing." Complexity is stressful and confusing. Simplicity is peaceful and straightforward.

- **Forgiving is better than getting even.**
  We should flush out all bitterness from our recollections. To forgive is to unload our mental burden. To carry the thought of revenge is like drinking poison and hoping it will kill the person who upset us.

- **Actively seeking knowledge is better than passively receiving it.**
  We must be responsible for our own learning throughout our lives, constantly seeking and applying knowledge and learning to think critically.

Be Driven by Results, Not Process

The nine simple guidelines are all about making choices that will help you become the person you want to be. Remember, though, when deciding how best to act, to focus on evaluating the consequences rather than analyzing the procedure. The approach to a task should be driven by the desired result. Be cautious of spending effort and resources on the process and overlooking the outcome.

In other words, pay attention to what you want to accomplish, not to the tool you'll use to accomplish it. Capturing memories is more important than the camera you are using. It's the fish you are going after, not the fishing rod.

Say you need to create a few holes and you must use a drill to make them. Your project calls for a specific size of drill bit that you don't have. Consider this: When you go to the hardware store, are you buying a drill bit or are you actually buying a hole?

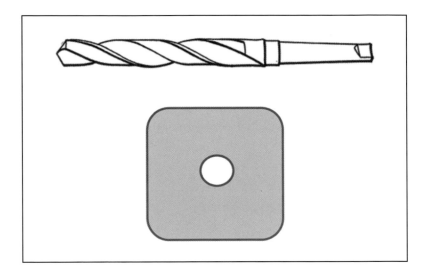

Drill Bit and Hole

1. Bottom in the Best Is Better

than Top in the Average

THIS GUIDELINE is about enriching our lives through better-quality associations.

During my high school years, I had to choose between two schools. One was less well-known, with a lower ranking and tuition, but it was very close to home and it would allow me to jump a grade. The other school was much better and higher ranked, but it was relatively far from home.

I chose convenience over quality. The benefit of being able to skip a grade to complete high school one year earlier seemed attractive, as did the greater proximity to my home. I felt strongly that learning depended on my own efforts, and not on the quality of the teachers or school. I had confidence that I could be an ace student in any educational setting. When I graduated as one of the top students in my high school class, I thought I had been proven right.

I learned the hard way that I was sorely mistaken when I received the results from the Government High School Exit Examination, which all graduating high school students had to take. Compared with all the high school graduates in Hong Kong, I was a below-average student. (*Below average?!*) Not only was this a blow to my pride and self-esteem, it was also one of the reasons I was rejected by Hong Kong's only university (at that time). Studying abroad was not affordable for me, so I was forced to get a job rather than pursuing a college degree.

My high school experience demonstrates how being higher up in a not-as-good group can look more appealing than being lower in a better group. Being near the top in any group gives us a sense of pride and satisfaction, regardless of the relative rank of that group. I felt proud to graduate in the top of my class!

But what we may not realize is that the comparative ranking of the group we associate with is more crucial than our position within that group. Even when we are near the bottom of a higher-ranked group, we are still a member of a better group.

When I chose that lower-quality high school, I overlooked the advantages of associating myself with schoolmates and teachers from relatively better social, family, and educational backgrounds. Most importantly, I did not recognize how my connections with those people might influence my life decades later. My decision to attend a mediocre high school was one I regretted for a long time. Had I applied this concept in my early teens, my life would have headed in a much more positive direction. Perhaps this is why I consider this to be the most important of all the guidelines (yes, in spite of telling you they are all equal!). This is the one that has affected my life the most.

Nowadays, I tell friends, relatives, and the younger generations, "Who cares if a person is the absolute worst student to graduate from Harvard (or Stanford, or Cambridge), they are still a graduate of a distinguished university—the bottom in the best." During their years of study, that person gets connected to a network of educators, schoolmates, and alumni from an outstanding educational institution. The life experience, education, and social connections they gain from that affiliation will prove invaluable for the rest of their lives.

Location, Location, Location

The benefit of situating oneself among the best was reinforced for me when I studied real estate investing. As I was preparing to buy my first home, I learned the truth of the real estate agents' mantra, "location, location, location." Among properties with comparable prices, those in better locations generally have a greater potential for appreciation and resale value. These houses further benefit from being surrounded by a better neighborhood.

This modern-day real estate truism is reflected in a Chinese legend about the great Zhou Dynasty philosopher Mengzi (also known as Mencius), who lived from 372 BC to 289 BC. When Mengzi was very young, his father died, leaving his impoverished mother to raise her son alone. In search of the best circumstances for the boy in their difficult situation, his mother moved three times. The first home was by a cemetery, the second near a market. The third home, near a school, was where she decided to settle, because the school served as an inspiration for lifelong learning. Through his resulting studies, Mengzi eventually became a great scholar—the most famous Confucian scholar after Confucius himself.

This story became one of the famous traditional Chinese four-character idioms, mèng mû sān qiān, literally translated as "Mengzi's mother, three moves." The idiom refers to the importance of finding the right environment for raising children. To me, it also illustrates the important idea that changing our environment can change our life.

A Chinese proverb relays the same truth: jìn zhū chì, jìn mò hēi (one who stays near vermilion gets stained red; one who stays near ink gets stained black). It is wiser to push a cart of gold than a cart of coal; you might not get any gold flakes on your clothes, but you won't get dirty. Cut negative influences from your life and surround yourself with positive people, because the people we spend the most time with may eventually shape who we become. (Motivational speaker Jim Rohn has suggested that we are the average of the five people we spend the most time with.)

When Options Seem Limited

We almost always have many choices. If it looks to you like your choices are limited, make sure you are not ignoring those that require effort, courage, or risk. Discover what is available and select the best.

But if it seems like you have little or no choice in selecting your group, you can still strive for the best in whatever groups are open to you. I always believe in "doing my best," whatever I am doing. When I went back to full-time study, I knew I was not qualified to enter Ivy League colleges. Nevertheless, I always did my best, graduating from each university I attended with a near-perfect GPA (grade point average).

Choose Quality

This "bottom in best" approach works in many areas of life besides choosing which groups we join. Aiming for the bottom of the best is equally as effective when buying a house, selecting a school, choosing a job, or buying an automobile or tool. Look for quality in all your choices, from what you buy at the store to where you go on vacation and what stocks you pick.

Beyond the fact that quality is "good," it also has a hidden value. Even though a higher-quality tool is usually more expensive, it will likely be cheaper in the long run because quality products tend to last longer. Similarly, at nearly the same price, the base model of a higher-quality brand automobile gives better (present and resale) value than a top-of-the-line model from a less reputable and less reliable brand.

How to Make the Best Choices

How do we know which group or product will be best for us? What steps could have saved me in my teen years from choosing the wrong high school? Whether we are choosing a group, a home, a school, or a product, there are three questions we can ask ourselves to guide us to the best possible choice:

- Do I have enough information?
- Is this a need or a want?
- What is the future impact of each option?

One of the surest paths to the wrong choice is acting on impulse. Asking ourselves these questions can help us slow down, analyze our situation, and make a wise and informed decision.

Do I Have Enough Information?

When we make impulsive decisions, we often lack information. To determine the quality of a group or product, I recommend doing a careful analysis, especially if you are making a choice whose outcome will be crucial to your well-being. A quick decision may be efficient, but it may not necessarily bring the best result. Seek advice from someone who has experienced similar situations. Do some research and gather more details about all the available options. Think long term. Consider the option of making "no choice"—of simply doing nothing. There is nothing wrong with taking the time to analyze or even waiting for the right solution to show up. Avoid making snap decisions.

When confronted with options, you could use something as simple as a pros and cons list. Or, if you're like me and you enjoy applying more scientific precision to your decision making, you could use a "decision matrix" that compares your options and their relative importance, or weight (see Appendix A for an example of a decision matrix).

Is This a Need or a Want?

When you decide to buy something, especially a high-value item, ask yourself whether it is a need or a want. We often buy unnecessary stuff by convincing ourselves that a toy is actually a tool, simply to justify its purchase. A decision should be based on needs, not wants. And if an item is indeed a necessity, then we should select it from the best group. To help us determine if an item is a necessity, we can ask, "Is it a tool or a toy?"

A tool is a device used to carry out a function. A toy is an object to play with, the main purpose of which is pleasure. Of course, we must have a few toys but we should not use *tool* as an excuse to buy any toy. Similarly, we should not disguise *want* behind a veneer of *need*. An automobile could be both a toy and a tool, but do we really need a luxury vehicle for our commute to work?

What Is the Future Impact of Each Option?

Our current choices and actions will always have an impact on us at some point in the future. We may think we are taking this into account when we make decisions, but sometimes we don't look far enough ahead—such as when I chose to attend a lesser-quality high school. I was thinking only as far ahead as graduation and not considering how it would affect my opportunities for college and beyond.

Two key financial concepts that can help us consider future impact are Return on Investment (ROI) and payback period. ROI measures the return on an investment relative to its cost. Payback period is the length of time it takes to recover the original amount. A higher ROI offers a shorter payback period. Really, this is a way of measuring how much you get out of a purchase or project relative to what you put into it.

Of course, we cannot measure everything in monetary units, so I also recommend using Return on Value (ROV). You can use ROV to assess concepts such as pride, knowledge, confidence, happiness, and satisfaction. For example, you could use ROV to evaluate whether, given the same expenditure of time and effort, you would achieve a higher level of satisfaction from writing a book, learning to play the piano, or learning to do portrait photography. You could also use ROV to evaluate whether or not the resulting satisfaction of something justifies its cost or effort. Is a $1,000 bottle of wine 10 times as satisfying than a $100 one? Do you *need* or *want* the expensive wine?

Measuring ROV means asking, "How much will my level of happiness or life enrichment increase compared to the amount of investment and effort I will make?" An analysis of ROI (or ROV) helps us choose the best option with maximum benefit.

Summary

- By associating with the best—for example, by joining a group of more educated people—you are inherently richer.

- Buy a home in the best neighborhood you can afford.
- Purchase high-quality tools and products that last.
- If you have to join a lesser-quality group, give it your best efforts. Aim to reach a higher level in whatever you do.
- Before you make any decision, do a careful analysis by asking yourself three questions:
  - Do I have enough information?
  - Is this a need or a want?
  - What is the future impact of each option, including return on investment or value?

2. Half-Full Is Better

than Half-Empty

The optimist sees the donut, the pessimist sees the hole.
—OSCAR WILDE

THIS GUIDELINE is about the advantages—and the many ways—of choosing optimistic thinking.

In my late teens and early twenties, I was what my American-born friends call an "unhappy camper." I paid too much attention to what I did not have. My schoolmates and friends seemed to have all the good stuff, and I wanted what they had. I especially envied people who had fancy home stereo systems with great amplifiers and speakers. The cost of such equipment was way beyond my reach, but I still visited stores to check out the latest hi-fi components, and my wish list grew increasingly lengthy. I told myself, "When I grow up, I am going to get myself everything on my list!"

Fortunately, I learned to turn my misery around. Instead of feeling inferior, I channeled my energy into doing something constructive to realize my dreams. I turned my wish list into intention and action. I'm proud that I have gradually fulfilled almost all those wishes from my late teens and early twenties. I now have one of the best hi-fi systems available set up in a dedicated, fully acoustic room where I spend many enjoyable hours listening to the music I love so much.

When we look at a half-filled drinking glass, we may ponder an age-old question: Is the glass half-empty or half-full? Of course, the answer depends on how we choose to view it. The drinker may see the glass as half-empty: "I need a refill." But the pourer might see it as half-full: "You still have half a glass of water, but I'd be happy to fill it up for you if you want more." Same glass, different perspective.

We naturally seek what we don't have. Our survival instinct and innate curiosity urge us to constantly look for novelty and new resources. But there is no end to this, because once one desire is satisfied, a new one replaces it.

Many of us wish we had more money, but are we happier when our income rises? A 2010 Princeton University study found that, as our annual income rises, we tend to become "happier"—that is, until that income reaches around $75,000, beyond which happiness does not change much. More income may simply mean more spending to satisfy more wants.

The best way to break this vicious cycle is to switch our focus from what we *lack* to what we have. It may be a cliché, but the expression "stop and smell the roses" makes a lot of sense. We own many things and are surrounded by plenty of beauty, all of it patiently waiting for our attention. When we have half a glass of water, why not call it half-full and enjoy every last drop?

The following points are some mental attitude shifts that can help us make this switch from half-empty to half-full.

Let Go of Expectations

I had quite an epiphany in one of my human behavior classes when we studied the concept of tempering expectation. In fact, I wondered how I had missed this for so long. The concept is simple: Keep all expectations in check, because "without expectation, everything is icing on the cake." For example, money we pick up on the street can seem sweeter than money we already have simply because we were not expecting it.

Practice Gratitude

We really have so much to be thankful for—possessions, wonderful surroundings, and all the good people near us. Most of all, I am thankful that I am still alive today. Many people did not make it. Especially as I get older, I treat every day as a bonus. Yesterday is gone and tomorrow is not here yet, so I do my best to enjoy the present moment and apply the power of now. When we practice gratitude, we are giving ourselves a gift.

Content Yourself with the Way Things Are

Many of us refuse to accept ourselves because we are not all we think we should be. This is another way of focusing on half-empty. I recommend accepting yourself as you are instead of how you wish you were. Focus on the full instead of the *empty*—all the wonderful qualities and things you have rather than what you lack. After all, isn't the *happiness of pursuit* better than *pursuing happiness*? The old Persian proverb "I cried because I had no shoes until I saw a man who had no feet" serves as a good reminder to count our many blessings.

Avoid Comparing Yourself with Others

A Chinese saying tells us, yī shān hái yǒu yī shān gāo, literally "there is another mountain higher than this one." This saying reminds us to be humble because there is always someone out there who is stronger, smarter, and richer. What hides behind this mountain could be an even larger one. The subtle message I take from this is to stop comparing myself with others.

Self-acceptance is a positive alternative to comparing yourself with others. First, accept who you are and what you have right now. Then, look for ways to become the person you want to be.

Compare Yourself with Your Own Potential

Why do some brands compare themselves with others, while other brands do not? For example, a TV commercial for KIA featured a comparison chart showing how one of its models performed better than BMW, Honda, and Nissan.[21] Does a superior product need to compare itself with the other brands? I don't think BMW has ever compared its products to KIA's. By comparing its brand with others, KIA unintentionally implies that it is the inferior brand. Their comparison leads me to think that if I were in the market for a new car, I should look at those competing brands. Even their competitor is mentioning them, so they must be better.

Don't fall victim to compare-and-despair syndrome. If you want to compare, go ahead. But compare yourself with yourself. Use your potential as a benchmark. Are you better off now than a year ago, or three years, or eight years? Have you fully lived up to your potential? How can you develop yourself to maximize your potential? Enrich your life experiences instead of your possessions. Life is like running a marathon: The important thing is that you complete it, not how fast you run compared to the other runners. As the saying goes, "Even if you win the rat race, you are still a rat."

Work with the Emptiness

Instead of bemoaning our half-empty glass while admiring another person's full one, perhaps we should find a way to fill it. This is what I did during my late teens and early twenties by writing down what I wished I had and drafting a plan of action to achieve those wishes.

Or, better still, why not get a smaller glass so the water you already have reaches the top? I did this too when I learned the benefits of simplicity and reorganized my life around my limited resources.

Or consider this: Unless we are very thirsty, do we even need a full glass of water?

When I was instructing Dale Carnegie courses, my mentor taught me a creative way to make a classroom look full. At the beginning of a session, if there were a few empty chairs, I would ask all the class members to stand and move forward into any empty chairs in front of them. Any empty chairs in the back were quickly removed, making the classroom look full.

Lesson learned: There is always a way to eliminate the emptiness.

Summary

- A positive attitude can make you healthier and happier.
- Turn envy into a plan and take action.
- Treasure who you are right now and what you already have, because chasing what you lack has no end.
- Keep your expectations in check and everything will be icing on the cake.
- Compare yourself only to your own potential.
- Learn to work and play with emptiness.

3. Walking Toward Is Better

than Walking Away

Always do what you are afraid to do.
—RALPH WALDO EMERSON

THIS GUIDELINE is about facing your problems, taking action, and finding the treasure in adversity.

Soon after I graduated from high school, I started work as a sales representative. With my lack of higher education and work experience, a sales job seemed to offer me the best prospects for income and opportunity. As I have already shared, my self-confidence was low due to some personal defeats, and I found myself dragging my feet to work every morning. I pushed myself very hard, but being an introvert, I was uncomfortable having to knock on doors and talk to strangers.

One day, I decided I had to face this problem head on, otherwise I would be a total failure, with no qualifications, no job, and no future. To help lessen my uneasiness about interacting with people, I began to attend sales training courses, read inspirational books, and listen to recordings by motivational speakers. I discovered that the best way to overcome fear is to confront it rather than to walk away from it. Truly, "nothing ventured, nothing gained."

Flight is one of our natural reactions to real or perceived hostilities. Why would we want to take unnecessary risks? But while flight seems like a safer and easier response than staying and "fighting," this avoidance can give us a false sense of relief. We often avoid objectionable situations, hoping they will go away. Sometimes they do, but more often they persist or even get worse.

In many cases, offense is the best defense—and by offense, I am recommending not so much fighting as facing. By facing our problem, we are more likely to solve it, thus eliminating the very source of our stress and gaining confidence in our abilities. As a bonus, we will also discover whatever opportunities are hidden in our adversity. I firmly believe that even the most problematic challenges yield plenty of opportunities. It is up to us to uncover them.

Imagine a beautiful pearl and how it begins as an oyster's natural reaction to a tiny grain of sand. The oyster creates layers of a material called nacre to protect itself from the irritation of this intruder, turning it into a gorgeous pearl. We, too, can make a "jewel" out of an irritating situation. In a much-quoted phrase, Elbert Hubbard, a Christian anarchist, summed it up perfectly: "When life gives you lemons, make lemonade."

Leave Your Comfort Zone

Early one morning on a recent RV trip to Santa Barbara with our friends Annie and Hung Ng, we were exploring the surrounding mountain trails. We drove in my Jeep Wrangler along a lengthy off-highway trail where none of us had ever been before. The sun was shining directly at us and we could not clearly see the path ahead. With no GPS signal, we got lost. It was quite scary going off the beaten path, but Hung's adventuresome spirit put our minds at ease. "Getting lost is part of the fun," he said. "We will explore more of the magnificent scenery by driving around to look for the right trails."

We live inside our comfort zone to avoid life's problems and challenges. By shying away from opportunities outside of our comfort zone, we miss valuable chances to gain knowledge and experience. By leaving our comfort zone and taking some prudent but uncomfortable risks, we stretch ourselves and add spice to our lives. If you choose to do nothing, you may minimize your mistakes, but you also miss out on so many potentially life-changing opportunities.

Confronting challenges and seizing opportunities will be a win-win because you win if you succeed *and* if you fail. But if you walk away—well, you most surely miss out. If you walk toward your challenges and opportunities, you will always be a winner. And every time you leave your comfort zone, you make it bigger!

Be Courageous

Ask yourself, is it really true that avoiding a risk or giving up an opportunity is playing safe? Isn't avoidance really more about weakness and laziness than being safe? Tackling life's problems and opportunities requires considerable courage and effort, so be brave.

A famous Chinese proverb about courage asks us bù rù hǔ xué, yān dé hǔ zi (If you don't enter the tiger's den, how will you get the tiger's cub?). There is no success without risk. High risks produce large rewards! If you are not afraid to take high risks, by all means go after the lucrative yields from options trading or the adrenaline rush from skydiving. Whatever level of risk you can tolerate, you will find the greatest treasure beyond what is merely comfortable.

Be Adventuresome

Try a new venture whenever possible. Do something different—or do what you usually do differently. Explore strange places. Travel the world, or play tourist in your own city, like I did before I left Hong Kong. Pick up interesting and challenging hobbies. Exposing yourself to new things offers you a refreshing break from life's routine.

Life is too short to miss out on all the fun stuff. I would rather feel sorry for having done something stupid than for missing the chance of doing it. You don't know until you try. Stop settling for the same old thing.

Be Tenacious

Confronting risks and seizing opportunities is uncomfortable for most of us. It's natural to feel apprehensive about the unknown. We feel safe and secure in our familiar environment. It takes conscious effort to expand our comfort zone, and we have to convince ourselves why we should.

Success does not generally result from first attempts. Oftentimes, it takes many iterations of trial and error. I urge you to never give up without a fight. But . . . first you have to jump into the ring.

Summary

- Walking away from problems can give you a false sense of relief (the problem is still there); facing them brings true relief.
- Walking toward problems, you are also walking toward opportunities.

- Confronting your problems requires risk and persistent effort, but the rewards are rich.
- There is no success without risk.
- Every time you leave your comfort zone, you expand it, so take on new experiences at whatever level of risk you can tolerate.
- Facing problems and seizing opportunities is a win-win; even if you "fail," you gain new opportunities and experiences.

4. The Present Is

Better than the Past

> *Be happy for this moment.*
> *This moment is your life.*
> —OMAR KHAYYAM

THIS GUIDELINE is about the happiness that comes from living in the moment.

In Hong Kong, I had many professionals among my closest friends. When I needed legal advice, I would just pick up the phone and talk to my lawyer buddy. My physician friend refused to accept any consultation fee from me when I visited him. My accountant pal gave me tax-strategy advice when we got together. I could easily get information from the government because I knew a few high-ranking officers who could refer me to the right person in the right department. These relationships were what I missed most after I came to California. In fact, relationships (*guanxi* in Chinese) are a crucial part of how business is done in most Asian countries.

During my early years in the U.S., I would frequently preface remarks to friends and family with, "Back when I was in Hong Kong . . ." and "I remember when . . ." I boasted about having my staff run errands for me, and how banks, retail shops, restaurants, post offices, and professional offices were all within a short walking distance. When I felt I was not getting the information I needed, I would say, "When I was in

Hong Kong, I knew someone who knew someone . . ." Soon, people around me got sick and tired of me bragging about the convenience of my old life.

One day, several questions flashed across my mind: Why am I still talking about Hong Kong all the time? Why am I living in the past? Isn't it true that what's passed is past? My past glories were meaningless to my new life, and my professional connections were no longer nearby. I knew it was doing me no good to live in my memory, so I decided to focus on the present and the future.

Choosing what to remember from our experience shapes how we project ourselves to the world today. This is why it is best to keep fond memories and let go of bad ones, though even lingering too long on past glories can paralyze our mind. Better to channel our energy into doing something pleasurable and appreciating the present moment.

I like to remind myself that, in English, the word *present* also means *gift*. This helps me appreciate the *existence* of the present moment because it truly is a gift. The past is gone forever, the future yet to come. Each day when we wake up, our lives start afresh. Many people did not make it to today, so every new day should be welcomed and celebrated. Smile and enjoy the day, because we never know when it is our last.

Be Open to Change

Change is the only constant in life. The key to enjoying *nowness* is to learn how to adapt to change. No two seconds, let alone days, are identical. Relish the present moment. Everything that happens now is a new experience, every second a new beginning.

Be a Change Driver

Accepting change does not mean being passive. You can also take charge and make change happen. Don't put off what you can do today. We cannot change the past, but we do have control over what we can do right now!

Be Realistic

The past is gone forever. Always thinking of our past achievements is not practical. Let bygones be bygones. The future is uncertain. We may envision it and make plans, but we should not spend too much time dreaming about it. Instead, do something today to make something happen. Only today is real.

Be Cheerful

Every day, find something you love to do. Being joyful is easier when you are doing things you love. Instead of reminiscing, rejoice in the present moment. Be grateful that you are here now, alive. Only the present has any real value. Be cheerful. Celebrate the day. Some people say TGIF—thank goodness it's Friday. I say TGIT—thank goodness it's today!

Summary

- Keep the lessons you've learned from the past and let go of the rest.
- Live in the present, because that is where you find true happiness.
- Be open to change, because it is life's only constant.
- Maintain a joyful attitude by finding something you love to do every day.

- Avoid reminiscing about your past glories or regrets.
- Focus on what you can achieve now, not on your past accomplishments.
- Welcome each day with open arms.

5. Money at Work Is

Better than You at Work

A penny saved is a penny earned.
—BENJAMIN FRANKLIN

THIS GUIDELINE is about putting money to work to build your personal wealth.

The day before I left Intuit, I had an interesting chat in the cafeteria with my colleague Dave. As Dave was handing me back my teacup, the only personal possession I had left from my office, I said:

Dave, you know I've always brought lunch to work throughout my 10 years at Intuit. I rarely buy lunch at the cafeteria or outside restaurant. Let me show you some numbers. I am using a moderately conservative figure of $20 a week in savings. This means that I am saving roughly $80 a month or $1,000 a year. In 10 years, I have saved a total of $10,000! Today, I am leaving Intuit with my teacup and a bonus check of $10,000.

I still vividly recall the grin on Dave's face. Of course, this "bring your lunch to work" plan is but a modest example that doesn't even factor in the money made from investing the unspent lunch money over the years.

If you remember only one thing from this chapter, remember this: It is not how much you *make* but how much you *save* that matters. One dollar saved could become two dollars (or more) earned, because the money you accumulate is earning additional money for you through the miracle of compound growth. This is the basic concept of money at work.

I will illustrate the power of compound growth with a very old tale about a king and the game of chess. Like many old stories, it is told in different ways, but perhaps the best-known version involves an Indian mathematician named Sessa who, according to the story, invented the game of chess.

One day, Sessa sat down with the king to proudly introduce him to his new invention. Unsurprisingly, the king became completely enthralled with the game—so much so that he proclaimed that Sessa should be given a very grand prize. Caught up in his glee, the king made a rare decision that Sessa could name his own reward, a truly unusual opportunity.

Sessa confused the king by asking for only a very modest prize: "Your Highness, I do not want money or jewels as a reward. I ask only for a chessboard with wheat placed upon each square, one tiny grain on the first square, two on the second, four on the third, and so on to the end of the chess board, and nothing more."

"A few grains of wheat?" the king scoffed. He was deeply puzzled by how Sessa could be brilliant enough to dream up such a fascinating intellectual game, yet so foolish as to choose such a paltry reward.

But of course, Sessa was no fool, as the king would learn when his court treasurers told him just how much wheat would be required to fill all 64 squares of a chess board. It turned out that the kingdom would be indebted to Sessa far beyond his or the king's lifetime. The king was incredulous. "How can this be?"

So, how many grains of wheat was Sessa asking for with his "modest" request? The math reveals the stupefyingly large number 18,446,744,073,709,551,615 (almost 18.5 quintillion). By comparison, a group of curious mathematicians at the University of Hawaii recently calculated the number of grains of sand making up all the beaches of the world as 7,500,000,000,000,000,000 (7.5 quintillion)—considerably fewer than the number of grains of wheat on Sessa's chess board.

In some versions of this story, Sessa was appointed the king's highest financial adviser. In others, he was executed for making the king look like a fool. (We don't know who actually invented chess, of course, but that's not the point of this story.)

For us, today, the main takeaway is that if we invest money and let it grow at a fixed rate for a period of time, the money will grow like the grains of wheat on Sessa's chess board. With only a little bit of care, your money can and will double in size at a regular rate. Eventually, the math will make your money grow beyond what you may think is possible in a normal lifetime.

The details of investing are outside the scope of this book (there are lots of great books you can refer to). My main concern is that you master the basics. This story of Sessa and the king lets you in on one of the most fundamental secrets of success. Use it to your advantage and you, too, can own a kingdom.

Capitalism

It is easy to overlook that the root of capitalism is *capital* (or money). A capitalist is a person who uses money to produce more money. To start this growth, we must first have seed money. Wealth is generally created with capital raised through the accumulation of liquid assets (investments easily turned back into cash), such as by saving and investing in stocks and bonds. The accumulation of these assets is the basis for prosperity, wealth, and financial freedom.

The Power of Accumulation

I recognized long ago that saving money is just as important as making money. My active and persistent savings habit helped me fulfill my goal of financial independence at an early age. I retired early and was able to enjoy freedom from financial worries. For many years now, I have been able to choose what I want to do without the burden of producing income from work. It is a simple fact that a few dollars saved each day can become a significant sum over time through compound growth—like wheat on a chessboard. The results can be truly surprising.

How much growth might you expect from smart investing? This depends on what stage of life you are in. In general, when you are younger and first starting to save, you'll want to look at the stock market, a tried and true method of building wealth over time. You will probably want to invest more cautiously as you get older and after you retire, since higher yields come with greater risk. After you have your nest egg, protect it by spreading your assets out into more income-producing investments (probably bonds) that are less volatile. Though they won't grow as quickly, they will produce a more reliable stream of income.

Given this simple strategy, you can reasonably expect your assets to grow at something like 7 percent (or even better, as history shows) during your growth years as you invest in stocks. During your retirement, or any time when you aren't working, your portfolio will be more conservative, so project your earnings with a much more modest rate of return—say 4 percent for your non-working portfolio, which is probably low enough to account for the effects of inflation (how dollars may decrease in value over time).

Protect yourself from the potential pitfalls of any one investment by diversifying your investments. To diversify your stock portfolio, consider using an index fund. Index funds offer you not only diversification, but generally low fees and tax efficiencies as well. Above all, make sure you have an understanding of what you invest in and that it suits your current goals and risk tolerance.

Never underestimate the power of the accumulation of money or the downright magical outcomes from the simple compound growth of prudent investments. For example, setting aside just $2.78 (a cup of coffee) a day at a 7 percent annual compound growth rate would result in a whopping $14,507.29 in only 10 years!

Saving Per Day	In One Month	In One Year	In 10 Years	In 20 Years	In 30 Years
$2.78	$83.33	$1,038.70	$14,507.29	$43,662.04	$102,253.20
$5.00	$150.00	$1,869.73	$26,114.17	$78,594.81	$184,063.12
$15.00	$450.00	$5,609.19	$78,342.51	$235,784.43	$552,189.37
$27.20	$816.00	$10,171.34	$142,061.09	$427,555.77	$1,001,303.39

Compound Interest Table

Referring to the last row of the table above, if you save $27.20 a day for 30 years at a 7 percent annual growth rate, you will end up with $1,001,303.39. With total deposits of $293,760.00, your money makes $707,543.39 for you. Notice that after 11 years, your monthly yield is larger than your monthly deposit; that is, each month your money is earning more than the amount you put in.

All from just prudent savings!

When I think of accumulation, I often recall the lyrics of a decades-old theme song from a TV show for kids sponsored by a Hong Kong bank:

As tiny as water droplets, together, they become sea and ocean; as minute as sand grains, collectively, they turn into wide earth.

What an excellent way to encourage kids to save money early in their lives.

Nest Egg

Let's say you use your growth years wisely and build a nest egg. How big is big enough? A financial nest egg of $1,400,000 with an average annual yield of 4 percent will produce a healthy $56,000 a year. A report published by the U.S. Census Bureau showed that the 2015 median annual household income in the United States was $55,775 ($64,500 in California). If your standard of living is on par with the median income in your area, a liquid asset of $1,400,000 ($1,600,000 in California) could generate enough income to give you the flexibility of not having to go to work. Instead, your money is working for you. As an added benefit, your net *take-home* pay is larger because investment income could be taxed less than wages.

Financial freedom should be the main goal of accumulating liquid assets. With enough money working on your behalf, you have the freedom to do what you want with your time. If you prefer to keep your job, you can do so by choice and not out of need. Your goal is not to avoid work, it is to live smartly so you create more life choices.

The Magic Number

So, really, saving is the key to financial freedom. Through the years I have enjoyed playing with the numbers to figure out how saving can yield great results. For example, I learned a bit of magic with the number 8.33. If you multiply 8.33 by 12, you will get 99.99, which you can round up as 100. Applying this magic number to a monthly savings of $8.33 is equivalent to saving $100 at the end of 12 months. Similarly, $83.33 a month (or $20.83 a week, or $2.78 a day) for 12 months becomes $1,000![22] Somehow, doesn't $1,000 seem to be quite a lot larger than just $83.33 multiplied by 12?

To make your savings magic happen, it is wise to adjust your spending habits. Actively seek to make changes that would help you save a meager $2.78 or more a day. Adopt the habits of driving fewer miles, brewing coffee at home, bringing lunch to work, avoiding late-payment fees, skipping alcoholic drinks when dining out, drinking water instead of soda, and avoiding credit card debt. Be vigilant about avoiding unnecessary extra-small charges. Save just a dollar here and a dollar there and pretty soon you are talking about big bucks! In less than 20 years, you might have enough money to buy a brand-new car or even more!

Uhmmm . . . come to think of it, had I worked at Intuit for 10 more years, on my last day I could have taken Dave for a joy ride in my new car bought with the lunch money I saved.

Be Meticulous in Managing Your Finances

Manage your personal finances vigorously. Your financial health is directly correlated to both your physical and mental health. Financial worry is among the top causes of stress for most of us. Part of being wise when it comes to personal finance is being ever-aware of the many psychological money traps and material temptations we can fall prey to. Sadly, financial responsibility is not generally taught in schools. Without basic knowledge of personal finances, most of us become victims of high interest payments, late-payment fees, additional charges, non-essential purchases, and poor investment decisions.

Advertisers like to use the word "savings" to entice us to buy. But how do you save when you spend? I remember a cartoon I saw a few years back. There is a poster next to on-sale merchandise with the words "SAVE UP TO 100%" followed by "WHEN YOU DON'T BUY ANYTHING."

How true! Saving and spending are mutually exclusive. A popular English proverb says it well: "You can't have your cake and eat it (too)." That is, you can't have your money and spend it too.

You don't have to spend money to verify having it. It is nice to enjoy the finer things in life, but don't spend your money simply to show off. Do you really want to buy things you don't need with money you don't have to impress people you don't like?

Personal Budgeting

The key to managing personal finances is budgeting. You must have a clear and current picture of how much you make and how much you spend. Personal budgeting gives you the information you need to make smart financial decisions. A budget also helps you control your spending through informed planning. The formula for the bottom line of a budget is actually quite simple:

$$\text{Total Income} - \text{Total Expenses} = \text{Surplus (or Deficit)}$$

Be knowledgeable about how interest works. People who understand interest earn it; people who don't understand interest pay it. There are two kinds of interest: Good interest is interest you earn; bad interest is interest you pay. Carrying debt is having interest working against you, the opposite of money at work. If you are paying interest, you are working for the money you owe. You become a slave to debt.

Avoiding consumer debt is vital if you want to achieve financial freedom. There is no reason to pay extra for something you buy. If you really need it and cannot immediately afford it, use what I call "reverse financing." Set up an account in which you set aside money regularly until the sum is enough for the purchase. I used this strategy to buy all my cars with cash and to raise enough cash for a down payment on my first condo.

While debt should generally be avoided, there are three exceptions where it may be a wise choice: home mortgage, education loan, and car loan. The cost of a mortgage for your home may be compensated by that home's appreciation in value; your monthly payments can also be treated as rent. Similarly, the interest on a student loan may be compensated by the increase in income a college degree can bring, making that interest an investment in a higher-earning future. If you are not able to buy a car with cash, the third exception is a car loan. When you need a car to commute to work, the interest is part of the cost of producing income. Remember to purchase a car that is commensurate with its purpose, though; you don't need an expensive sports car for commuting.

Be Frugal

A long time ago, a well-respected elderly lady who was my mentor told me: "When spending money, be mean to yourself but be generous to others, and not the other way around."

That was one of the best pieces of personal finance advice I have ever received, and I have done my best to follow it. What is meant by "be mean to yourself"? One way is to be frugal. Being frugal is a way of life, of avoiding wastefulness and being economical with your money.

Keep in mind that a dollar is a dollar. A dollar wasted is just as precious as a dollar earned. Before you spend money on anything, think of how hard it would be to earn that amount. Note that you have to earn slightly more than that amount, because you are taxed on your earnings. You would go a long way to save $10 on a $20 purchase. Would you do the same to save $10 on a $10,000 purchase? Why not? If you are lucky enough to find a $10 bill on the sidewalk, would you quickly spend it because it is not your money?

Be a Lifelong Saver

The accumulation of money has three components: period, yield, and amount of deposit. Of these three components, period is the most significant. The longer the period—the more time you allow your money to work for you—the larger your investment grows.

The Chinese four-character idiom kāi yuán jié liú (open source, block outflow) was originally used to describe tapping into a source of water while blocking its outflow to increase the level of a reservoir. This idiom is now often used in finance as a motivation for individuals and organizations to accumulate wealth and profits by increasing income and decreasing expenditure.

Start saving early and be a lifelong saver. Time is on the side of the young. If you start to save $9.00 a day at age 20 with a 7 percent yield, you will likely accumulate over a million dollars by the time you reach age 65. But though the math favors the young, remember that you are never too old to start!

Summary

- It is not how much you make but how much you save that matters.
- Financial freedom should be your main financial goal.
- Compound interest can turn savings of a few dollars each day into a significant sum over time.

- Having money and spending it are mutually exclusive.
- Manage your finances vigorously by budgeting and avoiding most consumer debt.
- Debt may be acceptable for a mortgage, student loan, or car (when it is transportation to work).
- Saving money regularly makes you feel more secure.
- Financial freedom gives you the freedom and flexibility to pursue your dreams.

6. Responding Is

Better than Reacting

*It's not what happens to you, but
how you react to it that matters.*
—EPICTETUS

THIS GUIDELINE is about mitigating confrontation by staying cool.

Of the nine guidelines, this is the one I find most difficult to follow. In some irritating situations, even though I try to stay calm, I just cannot control my temper. When my blood glucose levels drop (that is, when I am hungry), I get grumpy and short-tempered. This can trigger irrational and regretful actions toward my family and the people around me. I know I am reacting rather than responding. Fortunately, this lasts for only a few minutes. Rational thinking soon kicks in and I respond sensibly. I am working hard to correct this behavior. Yes, I will remind myself to keep cool!

Let's begin with the Chinese translation of the words *respond* and *react*. The two Chinese characters representing *respond* are huí yìng, meaning "return gently when counteracting." The characters representing *react* are fǎn yìng, "reverse harshly when counteracting." Both Chinese terms share the same second character, the common root word, yìng (counteract). The literal attributes of these two Chinese terms in *respond* are "counteracting gently" while in *react*, they are "counteracting harshly." These two Chinese terms describe very well the essence of the words *respond* and *react*.

There is actually a second version of the Chinese characters representing *respond* that does not have a precise translation in English: xiāng yìng means "rebound supportively when counteracting" or, literally, "counteracting supportively." What a beautiful concept. Wouldn't it be wonderful if, in any relationship, we not only responded, but did so with the intention of being supportive?

The Best Response Is Often No Response

Reaction is natural for all living things; it's an innate mechanism for survival. In some situations, pausing and deciding could be too time-consuming. Taking time to concoct a thoughtful response could even be risky, such as during an emergency, when we don't have time to stop and analyze our options.

However, in most non-emergency situations, reacting is not the best response. It does not allow us to evaluate our options and select the best one. This is especially true in a conflict situation.

Military strategist Sun Tzu tells us in his ancient Chinese military treatise, *The Art of War*, "The supreme art of war is to subdue the enemy without fighting."

	Responding	Reacting
Action	Active	Passive
Conflict	Soft	Hard
Control	Good	Poor
Mindfulness	High	Low
Impact	High	Low

A Matrix of Responding and Reacting

Reacting is losing control. Responding is taking control. We maintain the upper hand by not reacting. Perhaps the best response is to use restraint, stay cool, and take a break before taking any action.

On how to learn to respond, Leo Babauta, the creator of the Zen Habits blog, suggests that, "The main thing to learn is mindfulness and the pause."[23] When a response is shallow and mindless, it becomes patronizing. Perhaps a pause—a lack of response—is a better response. By staying cool, we are nobler.

Be Flexible

In some situations, life is not a zero-sum game; the result of win plus lose does not have to equal zero. That is, it doesn't have to be you win, I lose or you lose, I win.

$$\text{Life} \neq \text{zero-sum}$$

Letting someone else win does not mean losing. Sometimes we may have to lose in order to win. Let's look at an example of a win-win scenario from defensive driving. *Reacting* is when you honk, shout a curse, and shoot a dirty look at the driver who recklessly cut you off. Such an unpremeditated incident might escalate to road rage. Who knows what could happen next. *Responding* is when you keep calm, change lanes, or slow down to let the other car move ahead. Everyone is happy. The driver steers the car swiftly in front of you. You are safe and composed. It's a win-win.

Let's look at another example. *Reacting* is when you vigorously argue with your supervisor when he or she is being obnoxious and unreasonably demanding. Such a confrontation may jeopardize your future in an organization. *Responding* is when you keep cool and disregard your supervisor's unreasonable behavior. Everyone is happy. Your supervisor enjoys a few minutes of feeling superior. You keep your dignity and go back to work without being too upset. It's a win-win.

When I was in sales, I learned the importance of focusing on the main objective: to make a sale. There's no point in "winning the argument but losing the sale." In the defensive driving example above, arriving safely at your destination is your main objective. Just let the other driver win. In the workplace example, your objective is to have a pleasant work day. It doesn't matter who's more competent. Just let your supervisor win. If you continue to feel annoyed, you may want to consider aiming toward financial freedom that will release you from working under a boss (see "Money at work is better than you at work," page 101). While you are establishing your financial freedom, you may want to refer to the following message:

A Poster Produced by the
British Government in 1939

Be Empathetic

Try to see the world through someone else's eyes. If you were the other person, what would you do? In the defensive driving example above, the driver may have been in a hurry for a legitimate reason. Your supervisor may be having personal problems. You have no way of knowing unless you gather more information. It is easier to manage the rage by not reacting.

Summary

- Not reacting is a great way to soften a confrontation, just as a soft landing lessens the impact of a crash.
- Respond with the intention of being supportive.
- Pause and remember that the best response might be no response.
- You retain the upper hand in a conflict situation by controlling your own impulsive emotions, not the other person.
- Life is not a zero-sum game: letting someone else win does not necessarily mean that you lose.
- Try to see the world from the other person's perspective.

7. Simplicity Is Better than Complexity

> Simplicity is the ultimate sophistication.
> —LEONARDO DA VINCI

THIS GUIDELINE is about the gratification of keeping life simple.

Of the nine guidelines, this is the one I find most fascinating. For me, keeping things lean and simple is almost like playing a game. I often challenge myself to complete a task in the least possible number of steps, finish a project with the fewest possible tools, run errands with the least number of stopovers, or better still, get by without doing anything at all! I call this the *intelligently lazy* choice.

Simplicity is generally defined as the quality or condition of being clear or easy to do. However, the spirit of the word goes beyond that. A Zen proverb tells us, "Knowledge is learning something every day. Wisdom is letting go of something every day." Hence, the quality of simplicity could also include letting go of something. Lin Yutang, one of the most influential Chinese writers of his generation, referred to this quality as the elimination of nonessentials.[24]

Very early in my pursuit of knowledge of management science, I found the topic of operations management particularly captivating. Known as organization and methods (O&M), it was developed as part of the British practitioner tradition during the mid-twentieth century as a process of assessing the efficiency and effectiveness of a company and implementing an optimal management system.[25] I found that many O&M system designs could be adopted by an individual—for example, I started using a stack of index cards and three-ring binders to organize my life.

One of the common goals of organizations is to keep their operations efficient and effective to enhance stakeholder value. Doing the *right things* is inherently easier when there are fewer options to choose from—a key characteristic of simplicity.

When I began my career as an insurance agent 50 years ago, I was inspired by a presentation given by Frank E. Sullivan.[26] As part of the presentation, he elaborated on the following three stages of professional development:

First stage: Starry-eyed enthusiasm
Second stage: Complicated sophistication
Third stage: Mature simplicity

A professional who reaches the mature stage has evolved from the earlier phases of enthusiasm and sophistication. The highest level of professionalism requires competency in simplicity and execution—doing the *right thing* right and doing it *right* the first time.

Simplicity Is Not Simple

It isn't always so obvious that doing something simple is preferable to doing something overcomplicated. Oddly enough, simplicity is not simple! Personal or business systems that start out small can grow like branches on a tree; close relationships and social connections inevitably become more tangled.

Things can multiply like bacteria or rabbits.[27] With the passage of time, something simple often morphs into something unwieldy.

Simplicity is about efficiency. It is easy to get lost in the middle of a busy city. Similarly, it is easy to get confused if we are reading a complicated set of instructions like the United States Internal Revenue Code. In 1913, the first Federal Income Tax Form 1040 was only four pages long, including the instructions; the current code has approximately 4 million words.

Whether it is an artistic movement or life philosophy, minimalism is marked by the same core tenet of simplicity. Minimalists believe that less is *really* more, and that having fewer possessions and obligations leaves them with more time to enjoy the essentials of life. After all, one can only eat so much at one meal, or wear one set of clothes, sleep in one bed, or take one form of transportation at a time. Why add more to enough?

Look at some of the hilarious cartoons created by Rube Goldberg.[28] He is famous for drawing machines deliberately over-engineered to perform a simple task, usually in some sort of extra-complicated chain reaction. Funny for what they are, those drawings also deliver some subtle lessons. How often do we unknowingly overcomplicate a task (or a relationship) in our lives? Can't life usually be easier than it is?

While it is wise to nurture efficiency, I caution against the false efficiency of multitasking that has recently emerged in modern life. Modern technology has made available many convenient tools that allow us to perform several tasks concurrently. However, research has repeatedly shown that while multitasking "feels" like it is saving us time, it is very inefficient.[29] Our brains just don't function that way. Beware of trying to focus on more than one task at a time; you are likely slowing everything down and achieving much less than you realize.

Be More Productive by Doing Nothing

Being a high achiever often comes with added stress. This is why I consider the ability to take a break to be an essential skill. Sometimes we end up being more productive when we take time to simply do nothing at all. Always set aside time off to enjoy the peace you deserve. This may mean saying no to others; think of it as saying yes to yourself.

Less Is More

An excessive accumulation of material belongings can contribute to life's complexity. Before taking possession of anything, consider the concept of "total cost of ownership," which goes beyond the purchase price. Ownership often comes with many extra costs, such as maintenance, service, licensing, tax, storage, and time. Consider, too, the opportunity cost, or loss of potential gain from other alternatives when one is chosen.

I wonder sometimes, *do I own stuff or does stuff own me?* Consider all the time and attention you put into the care of all your stuff (it might be more than you think!). Then ask yourself: Do I truly want to be a slave to my belongings? Think about this every time you shop and find yourself wishing you had that new cool thing: How long does it stay cool? Where will I store it? Do I need to keep it clean? Does it take up more space in my closet?

Simplicity is also about relieving ourselves of excess mental burden. When we accept more commitments and responsibilities than we can handle, fulfilling them can be quite stressful. We should therefore choose quality instead of quantity.

My colleagues at Intuit as well as at National University all noticed how *clean* my office always was. On my office desk, other than the computer and its peripherals, my only personal item was a porcelain teacup. Once I heard an Intuit colleague from a different department asking around about why my office was so empty. She was wondering if I had left. "No, he is still working here," she was told.

To me, it is much easier to take care of an assignment or analyze a problem if I have only one task in front of me on my desk. I can always do more with less clutter around me. My mind can focus on one thing at a time.

Having more of everything is not really "more" if we have less time to enjoy and take care of it all. For me, negligence of the things I have worked hard for is just a waste.

Less is also more in verbal and written communication. When you convey a message, do you want to impress or to express? In most situations, it is far more effective and sincere to express than to impress. Keep that in mind in your relationships, friendships, presentations, and even job interviews.

Be Efficient

Efficiency is all about maximizing productivity with the least amount of wasted effort. If tasks become too complicated, your precious efforts may be spread thin or wasted. Unless the goal is to enjoy the drive, the fastest route to a destination may not be the scenic route. The bees know better. That's why we call a straight line between two places a beeline.

Let Go of Physical and Mental Burdens

Letting go of excess physical and mental burdens is an important step toward leading a simpler life. When I think of "letting go," I think about things I can do to help make my life much better in the long run. Leo Babauta presented many creative recommendations on this subject in his essay "Simple Living Manifesto: 72 Ideas to Simplify Your Life."[30] Here are two of Babauta's steps:

- Identify what's most important to you.
- Eliminate everything else.

Acknowledge a loss if it is something beyond your control. Accept your losses and move on. In a way, our losses are helping us simplify our lives. In fact, we benefit from being able to let go of even positive experiences. The following anonymous quote makes a lot of sense: "If you love something, let it go. If it comes back to you, it's yours forever. If it doesn't, then it was never meant to be."

Summary

- Having fewer options to choose from is a key to simplicity.
- Doing the right thing is easier when you have fewer options.
- Simplicity is not always simple; beware of the tendency to overcomplicate.
- Simplicity is about efficiency, but avoid multitasking, as it actually slows things down.

- Maximize your productivity by taking time out to do nothing.
- Less is usually more, so keep your possessions, commitments, and communication as simple as possible.
- Let go of what no longer serves you.

8. Forgiving Is Better
than Getting Even

THIS GUIDELINE is about attaining serenity by lightening your mental load.

Mastering the virtue of forgiveness is truly challenging. It certainly has been for me. Whenever a person or situation provokes me, I tend to react negatively and feel uneasy. My throat becomes dry and my heart beats faster. Most of the time, I do my best to hide my reaction, but it's all too easy to carry the resentment with me.

Letting go can be a real challenge. Even when I try to forgive and forget, an uncomfortable scenario can keep swirling around in my head. I realize my bitterness and anger are caused by my own reaction rather than the painful event. While I know that I am free to let go, often I just can't. Sometimes it feels almost impossible to "get the monkey off my back."

Fortunately, my resentment generally doesn't last long. In most cases, within a few days I regain my usual positive attitude. Resentment is like the common cold. There is no instant cure, but eventually the symptoms disappear on their own. Sometimes, I wish there were a delete key I could press to erase an entire troubling incident from my memory.

Reject Resentment

There's a famous Buddhist fable about the price of clinging to feelings of resentment:

Two monks, an elder and a younger, were walking silently side by side on their way to a neighboring monastery. Along the way, they met a young woman crying softly on the bank of a river that the monks needed to cross. The woman turned to the younger monk and softly pleaded for help so that she could safely cross the stream and not ruin her dress.

The young monk shrugged and said to the woman, "I am a monk who has taken a vow of chastity. Unfortunately, I simply cannot help you."

But the older monk extended his hand with gentle compassion and said, "Climb on my back, and I will carry you safely across the river."

After reaching the opposite bank, the elder monk set the woman down on a dry patch of grass. Now smiling, she thanked the elder monk profusely and walked on her way.

The two monks continued their journey, again walking side by side in silence, but now the younger monk was becoming increasingly agitated. When they reached the monastery, the younger monk turned to his elder and said sternly, "You should not have carried that woman on your back. It is against our rules of chastity!"

The older monk calmly replied, "The young woman needed our help, and I simply carried her on my back to the other side of the river. But you, my friend, you have carried her all the way back to the monastery."

The moral of the story: Let go of your grudges. Put down your mental burden and move on.

There's a Chinese seven-word idiom, dé ráo rén chù qiě ráo rén, that literally means, "let people off easily when possible." In the end, forgiveness is a gift to ourselves, because resentment hurts us more than the other person. There is a saying: "Resentment is like drinking poison and then hoping it will kill your enemies." How true!

Ask yourself, "Do I want to carry around unnecessary mental baggage? Is it helpful to relive a past disappointment over and over in my mind? Am I content to live with anger or resentment sitting on my shoulder?" Thinking too much about a perceived or actual disturbing event only upsets us more. When you forgive, you are offering yourself a double plus of neutralizing your own negative feelings and paving the way for better relationships.

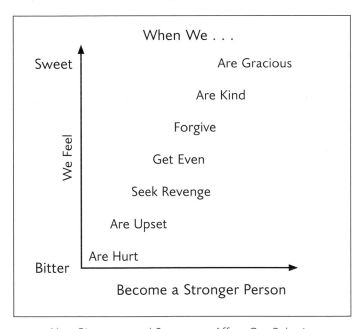

How Bitterness and Sweetness Affect Our Behavior

Success Is *Not* the Best Revenge

Is it necessary to seek revenge? Are there any real benefits to revenge?

The answer to both questions should simply be no. Why? Because we become better people when we don't seek revenge. The truth is, it takes a strong person to forgive. If the feeling of revenge is sweet, in the end the feeling of forgiveness will be even sweeter.

"Success is the best revenge." *Seriously?* Won't that kind of success feel hollow? Shouldn't we enjoy our success for its own rewards?

Doing the best is better than *being* the best. Who cares if someone is better than us? There is little point in measuring yourself against another person's yardstick (or one based on social norms). Compete against yourself, not others, by looking for ways to maximize your own potential. Ask yourself what you could do to become a better person than you were a few months ago, a year ago, or a few years back. When you are busy improving yourself, the thought of revenge will dissolve into trifling nonsense. You will simply have no time to waste on thinking about "getting even."

Be wary of using success to lash out at others in retaliation for your feelings of resentment. Success is indeed a noble goal, but don't use it for showing off or for retaliation. Very few people think or care about our "success." Of those who do, our success will arouse jealousy in many of them rather than admiration. I always recommend that we keep our successes to ourselves and savor them internally (and I do so myself!).

To forgive does not mean to forget. Treat your troubling episodes as lessons learned. Stay away from aggressive people and hostile situations as much as you can. Ignore them. As the saying goes, "Upset me once, shame on you. Upset me twice, shame on me." Just let it go.

Get Even with Kindness

The social norm of reciprocity is the expectation that we should treat people in kind. The idea of "getting even," for example, is a form of reciprocity. However, as I see it, getting even does not have to mean retaliation or revenge. In a positive way, it could mean doing something equally good to those who have been good to us. Find ways to pay back with good intentions.

A favor returned is an act of graciousness. The characteristics of graciousness include being humble, compassionate, polite, and respectful. A gracious person comes off as an elegant person.

A Chinese folk saying tells us, dī shuǐ zhī ēn, dāng yāng quán xiāng bào (a drop of water taken as a favor should be repaid with the amount of a surging spring). Literally, it means kindness should be repaid many times over. When we owe someone a favor, why not *get even, and then some?* Better still is to be kind even to those who mistreat us. When we do that, we are offering ourselves a double plus: the first is to neutralize our own negative feelings and the second is to pave the way for a better relationship.

A drop of water is more precious when we are dying of thirst. Teresa and I are forever grateful to Betty and Raymond, the couple who extended significant help to us during our hardship years. They are also among the few people who never looked down on us.

Be Assertive, Not Aggressive

If your actions are all about satisfying your own needs, you are being aggressive. If you let others take advantage of your needs, you are being too easy-going. You are assertive when your actions satisfy both your needs and the needs of others at the same time.

Temper your feelings toward others, and toward your own wins and losses. Don't over-celebrate your victories or excessively mourn your losses. The legendary UCLA basketball coach John Wooden wisely taught his teams that there should be no excessive approbation or dejection on the court after a win or a loss.[31] This is the essence of good sportsmanship and of being an emotionally balanced individual.

Stand up for your beliefs, but don't step over the boundary into being aggressive. Be assertive when you are right. The best defense is a good, gentle offense.

Of course, we often get irritated by aggressive people. If you are dealing with an aggressive person who is right, try to accept their opinion courteously. If you feel they are not right, present your facts calmly. If they are grossly irrational (let's face it, this can happen sometimes), simply stay away. Fueling aggression with aggression only sets up a chain reaction of increasing fury that can end in suffering or even tragedy—all avoidable by tempering your behavior.

For example, in a confrontation, arguing about facts is counterproductive. If you are right, and you know that the facts to back you up will eventually come to the fore, there is no point in pursuing the argument. Those who feel inferior generally want to win, regardless of the facts. Play down the importance of ego. The great speaker and trainer Dale Carnegie reminded us to make the other person feel important. Sometimes, we must lose to win.

Kindness Will Always Prevail

Be gracious. Kindness is the lubricant of the intricate gears of human interactions. Kindness is rewarded with happiness; a kind person is a happy person. Reciprocate with compassion when confronted by aggressive people and you may be surprised by the positive outcome.

The classic Zen koan, "What is the sound of one hand clapping?" provokes deep thinking about its meaning. If it takes two hands to perform a clap, then one hand clapping should produce the sound of *silence*. (Thank you, Simon and Garfunkel!) One hand clapping means the other hand is not hitting back. When we forgive the person who slaps us and refuse to retaliate, we are rewarding ourselves with peace of mind.

Summary

- Letting go of resentment is a great way to achieve peace of mind.
- By carrying thoughts of bitterness and retaliation, you are hurting only yourself.
- Forgiving gives you the double plus of relieving your negative feelings and improving your relationships.
- In the end, forgiveness feels sweeter than revenge.
- Achieving success as a form of revenge will never feel as good as achieving it for its intrinsic rewards.
- Use "getting even" as a form of reciprocity, and get even with kindness.
- Being assertive means satisfying your needs and the needs of others at the same time.
- Being gracious and kind will reward you with peace of mind.

9. Actively Seeking Knowledge Is

Better than Passively Receiving It

Live as if you were to die tomorrow.
Learn as if you were to live forever.
—MAHATMA GANDHI

THIS GUIDELINE is about the power of pursuing and applying knowledge throughout our lives.

I have always been passionate about learning. Libraries are
my favorite places to visit. I enjoy spending time there tremendously. Most of this book was written in two college
libraries. Shortly after I arrived in California three decades
ago, I began spending a lot of time in the public library near
Mom's house. I read many books on finance, investment, real
estate, and self-improvement. The knowledge I gained would
prove extremely useful when, a few years later, I began to
invest in real estate. The messages and inspiration in the self-
help books encouraged a positive outlook that carried me
through my challenging hardship years.

I also consider myself lucky to be bilingual. Being proficient in a second language opens my mind to wisdom from
diverse cultures. No translation can precisely match a word's
connotations and underlying implications. Reading a book
in its original language gives us a greater appreciation of the
book's subtext. Exposure to diverse cultures also gives us
broader views and philosophies of life.

For many years after I graduated from high school, I attended classes in judo, Chinese calligraphy, Chinese chess, piano, woodworking, and Cantonese. When I was reading the news at Hong Kong's largest television station, I employed a language professor to teach me to pronounce Cantonese words perfectly. A few years prior to my emigration, I put in a great deal of time and effort to qualify as an instructor for Dale Carnegie courses. As a hobby, I taught myself computer programming. I studied U.S. taxes as part of the curricula of the Chartered Life Underwriter (CLU) program. Little did I know at the time that this pursuit of learning would help turn my hardship years in the U.S. toward success.

Life Is Short, So Make It Count

It can be sobering to count our estimated average life expectancy at birth in days instead of years. Somehow, expressed in days, life can seem shorter. On average, we are born with approximately 30,000 days to live. This means a middle-aged person has about 15,000 days remaining.

Shouldn't we make good use of what's left?

Since we arrive on this planet without an owner's manual, we spend a great deal of our lives learning about ourselves, how things work, and how to interact with other people. We have to learn to recognize faces, walk, and talk. As we acquire and process information, we gradually create our own version of an owner's manual and gain knowledge about ourselves and our environment from experience, school, and the people we meet.

The Chinese term for "knowledge" is composed of two characters: xué wèn. Literally, the first character signifies *learn* and the second character signifies *ask*. This term could therefore be construed as "to learn and to ask." Asking is indeed the key to building knowledge. This is what I mean by *active* learning, rather than just passively taking in information. Preschool kids like to ask a lot of questions, but somehow by middle school, they tend to stop asking. To become a learned person, we should stay inquisitive like a preschooler. Nowadays, with the unlimited availability of information through technology, we can easily find answers to almost anything. At the same time, we should be careful about what we read.

Knowledge, benevolence, and courage were three virtues taught by Confucius. Referring to knowledge, he elucidated, zhì zhě bù huò (the one who knows does not go astray),[52] meaning that a person with knowledge and good judgment has the tools to differentiate between delusion and reality.

Critical Thinking

With so much information available to us now, it is imperative that we know how to think critically. Critical thinking is the ability to analyze information objectively and rationally so we can make informed decisions.

Traditionally, one of the best places to be introduced to critical thinking has been a college, university, or other institution of learning. But we need to do more than simply understand a concept. As British philosopher and sociologist Herbert Spencer reminds us, "The great aim of education is not knowledge but action." Critical thinking is the ability to evaluate facts and to better understand the world around us so we can intelligently choose what to believe and how to act.

With so many institutions of higher learning now leaning toward vocational training and professional development, we risk diminishing the importance of critical thinking. Newspapers now rate college degrees on their future earning potential and job opportunities, but a formal education should also train students to think critically—a skill that will surely serve them all their lives, in every domain.

Being able to think critically can help us become smarter. It can help us to filter out misinformation and dispose of useless noise, and to use reasoning, logic, and evidence to substantiate and refine our beliefs.

Never insist on your viewpoint when you don't have enough knowledge about a subject. Don't be afraid to admit you don't know something and need to find out more. When confused, investigate further to educate yourself. If we persist in pretending we are certain when we don't know the facts, we close our mind and limit our ability to make smart decisions.

From a critical thinking class, the group of topics I found among the most interesting were logical fallacies and their examples. Recognizing common errors in reasoning helped me examine my own thinking and become a cautious skeptical thinker. The logical fallacy that impressed me most is the fallacy of *post hoc, ergo propter hoc*. This is a Latin phrase for "after this, therefore, because of this." As intelligent people, we would do well to remember that correlation does not imply causation—in other words, we should avoid jumping to the conclusion that because one event happens after another, the first event caused the second. Somebody once said, "If you sneeze and it begins to rain, should you believe that sneezing causes rain?" We should verify whether two events are causally related. This fallacy is at the root of many superstitions and false beliefs. Once we recognize it, we can be more aware of the blunders of *ignorant certainty* and form more rational opinions.

Constantly Uncover the Truth

The sad reality is that the world is full of propaganda and lies. Even when facts are cited to back up a claim, the facts themselves can be tailored to serve specific aims. Marketers manipulate data to exaggerate the benefits of their products and services. Companies maneuver the numbers to achieve budgets. Historians present the victor's version of events. Politicians distort statistics to keep their jobs. Governments boast of accomplishments to hide failures.

This subject reminds me of an incident that happened when Mary-Ann, my youngest daughter, was almost two years old. At that time, I was a part-time newscaster at Television Broadcasts Limited, Hong Kong (TVB). I read the early morning news on weekdays and the noon news on weekends. One day, in closing the noon news, I presented myself professionally in front of the video camera with a smile and announced, "Finally . . . the latest about the local weather conditions. The clouds have moved away. We will have sunny skies for the rest of the day. Goodbye." I thanked the cameramen inside the studio and left for home. As I was walking back to my apartment, which was just a block from the television station, the rain began pouring down! When I stepped inside my apartment, I was as wet as a mop dipped in a sink. Mary-Ann giggled, "Daddy, Daddy, you lie, you lie!" I was speechless. Mary-Ann was too young to understand that I had to read, word-for-word, the script given to me by the news editor. In some situations, we do not have any freedom over the words we can say or the message they can express.

Finding truth can be tough, as we all have biases. Our values and beliefs are shaped by the people around us, our culture, and our upbringing. We all have our unique viewpoints, particularly on sensitive topics such as sex, religion, and politics. Most people try to stay away from openly discussing any of them.

It's ironic that some people:

- Practice sex, but they don't talk about it.
- Talk about religion, but they don't practice it.
- Don't talk about or practice politics—they just avoid it.

It is crucial to know how to differentiate between fact and fiction, as well as between reality and imagination. We should aim to always seek the truth through gathering information and drawing on our own knowledge and innate wisdom. Otherwise, we let others control us. Dictators use censorship to control the flow of information and keep hold of their power. Authoritarian governments control the minds of their citizens by limiting dissemination of and access to information. According to the United Nations Universal Declaration of Human Rights, "Everyone has the right to . . . seek, receive and impart information and ideas through any media and regardless of frontiers."

The following diagram is commonly used to describe the relationships among d̲ata, i̲nformation, k̲nowledge, and w̲isdom. Hence, it's called the DIKW hierarchy:

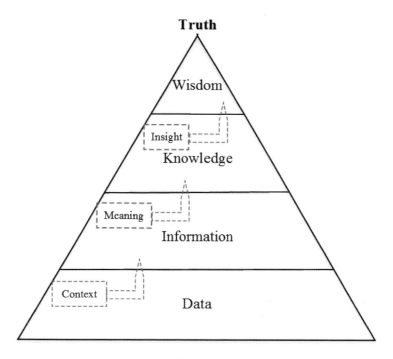

The DIKW Hierarchy[33]

Due to the information revolution, the sheer volume of data and information available can be unmanageable. We need to sift through what is out there and sort it into actionable knowledge. Data with context becomes information. Information with meaning becomes knowledge. Knowledge with insight becomes wisdom. Truth is the ultimate value of wisdom. We simply can't be a wise person without embracing truth.

Beware of lies and deceit. Some people blindly accept a claim even when there is not enough evidence to support it, but extraordinary claims need extraordinary evidence. When a very odd but favorable random event happens, some people say it is a miracle. If an odd random event is not desirable, should they therefore say it is a *disastrous coincidence?*

The difference between the truth and a lie is that, as new evidence is uncovered, what was previously accepted as truth can be changed or rejected. A lie can never be changed, because it will self-destruct. When the truth is challenged, more independent findings will further confirm its accuracy; when a lie is challenged, more lies must be introduced to cover it up.

Practice Lifelong Learning

As change is the only constant in life, we must continually update our practical knowledge and skills. There is a Chinese seven-word idiom that tells us yī xī shàng cún shū yào dú (with one last breath remaining, books must be read). That is, if we are still breathing, we must read and learn. Education gives us the foundation of knowledge. A college graduation ceremony is called commencement because it marks the beginning of a stage in life, not just the end. It is up to graduates to pick up the mission of learning from then on. Learning is for life.

Be Creative

To be creative generally refers to the ability to use ingenuity or innovative concepts to produce something. Creativity does not come from acquired book knowledge.

According to Sir Ken Robinson, schools don't always do a decent job of teaching and nurturing creative skills.[34] These skills are crucial in helping students adapt to an ever-changing environment. We should all become more creative. One way to accomplish this is to challenge conventional wisdom and seek alternative ways of doing things.

When others say, "Why?" we should say, "Why not?"

Challenge Conventional Wisdom

"The majority is always right" could well be dead wrong. Be skeptical. Have the courage to challenge conventional wisdom. Ask if things could be done differently. Give serious thought to the idea of thinking out of the box. Adjust your mindset. There is indeed "more than one way to skin a cat." (Sorry, *cats!*)

Could This Be Done Differently?

Look for alternatives:
- Could we start this procedure from the end? (A project is designed backward from the date of completion.)
- Could we turn it upside down? (A wine glass is made to look upside down.[35])
- Could we put it on inside out? (An inverted Hawaiian shirt is made inside out to create a faded look from the floral design.[36])
- Could we use this product for a different purpose? (A box of baking soda is used as an odor absorber.)
- Could we use this tool for a different purpose? (A pair of chopsticks is used to create a hair bun.[37])
- Could we reverse it to carry out our goal? (Money is set aside systematically to achieve a target amount.)
- Could we eat dessert first? (Someone near the dessert buffet is heard to say, "Life is short!")

Use brainstorming or mind-mapping techniques to generate ideas.[38] Ideas often breed more ideas. "Two heads are better than one." More minds breed even more ideas. (There are computer programs available for simplifying the process of creating mind-maps and conducting brainstorming sessions.[39])

The Need for Practical Knowledge

Knowledge is not just what you pick up from school and from reading books. It also refers to practical knowledge about what to do and how things work. We need to acquire the tools and skills to adapt to our changing environment. Practical knowledge should be constantly updated and refreshed to meet the changes we are facing.

The table on the facing page offers some examples of the practical knowledge we ought to acquire based on the Chinese golden rule of the four basic needs of life (clothing, food, shelter, transportation) during acquisition, maintenance, improvement, and disposition. Practical knowledge greatly enhances our quality of life.

Very few of these skills are learned at school. Actively pursuing these kinds of practical knowledge will give us the tools and skills we need for adapting to our ever-changing environment.

Basic Needs of Life / During	Clothing (Appearance)	Food (Meal)	Shelter (Lodging)	Transportation (Commuting)
Acquisition	• Shop for clothes • Buy cosmetics	• Get nutritional information • Find a restaurant • Shop for groceries	• Buy a house • Rent a house • Find a roommate	• Buy a car • Use public transportation • Organize a vacation
Maintenance	• Create a wardrobe • Maintain and store clothes • Personal grooming	• Eat healthily • Exercise	• Clean and maintain home • Set up and use home electronics	• Change oil • Check tire pressure • Wash car
Improvement	• Dress well • Apply make-up • Develop a sense of style	• Grow food • Adopt a vegetarian diet • Drink more water	• Landscape yard • Renovate house	• Upgrade car • Get a hotel upgrade • Use frequent flyer miles
Disposition	• Declutter home or office • Donate clothes • Hold a garage sale	• Lose weight • Get rid of bad eating habits • Recover from illness with herbal medicine	• Prepare a home for sale • Exchange rental properties • Sell a home	• Trade in old car • Donate old car

Practical Knowledge Examples

Summary

- We make the best use of our lives by engaging in lifelong learning.
- Taking in information is not enough; we must learn to think critically, challenge what we are reading or hearing, and discover the truth for ourselves.
- Have the courage to challenge conventional wisdom.
- Acquiring practical knowledge equips us to adapt to change.
- Apply your knowledge and skills to create something.
- Make it a habit to ask: Could this be done differently?

Part Three

EFFECTIVE GOAL SETTING:

A BALANCED APPROACH

Introduction: The Life-Changing

Practice of Setting Goals

DURING MY TWENTIES, I fell into a period of deep despair following one of the heartbreaking experiences I mentioned in Part One. For several months, I felt no purpose, no sense of direction, no meaning in life. I didn't even want to get out of bed in the mornings. Having no higher education and unable to go overseas for studies, I saw a bleak future ahead of me. Even my food seemed tasteless.

I felt hopeless. But one day, an idea came to me like a bolt of lightning: I could change my life.

I launched into a diligent search for answers. I didn't want to be this person who couldn't get out of bed, so I made a special effort to get up at 6:00 every morning. Slowly, I began to take control of my days.

The goal-setting practice I've followed ever since then was born from this simple (but not easy) recognition that I could—I must—take responsibility for my own destiny.

Many people spend more time scheduling a vacation than planning their lives. If you are not managing your life, you are just drifting. A goal without a plan is just a wish. As Benjamin Franklin said, "If you fail to plan, you are planning to fail!" Without goals, you are going nowhere.

You can't always make your life longer, but you can make it broader. By "broader," I mean unlocking your life to open it up to richer experiences. Goal setting is the key to broadening your life. Not only does it help you actualize your dreams, it also increases the quality and meaning of your life. Goal setting gives you a mission, a sense of purpose. It creates the drive and enthusiasm you need to turn your wishes into goals and then achieve those goals.

A Time-Tested Approach to Goal Setting

Goal setting has been my life. This book is the result of many years of dedicated study, education, mentorship, teaching, and experience. For over 40 years, without fail, I have sat down within days of my birthday, and again six months later, to revise, fine-tune, and update my goals. I also revisit them at times of change and transition, such as when I moved to the United States. The method of goal setting I am introducing to you here is exactly what I have used nonstop, year after year. More than any other practice, it has helped me become the person I want to be.

I was fortunate to recognize the need for setting goals early in my life. If you are able to begin as a young person, good for you. You will be setting (and keeping) your life on a positive course. But, if you are coming to goal setting later in life, do not be discouraged. As I said about saving money, it's never too late to start. Or, put another way, better late than never. There is no more powerful practice than defining who you want to be and planning consistent action, no matter what age you begin.

You may already be setting goals without realizing it. Vacation planning and saving for a down payment on a house are examples of setting goals. The idea now is to make your planning more structured and to cover all your bases by making sure your goals are "balanced"—that is, that you have goals in every important area of your life and that they are all working together.

You might be wondering: Why another book about set-ting goals? Haven't we all heard about SMART goals and the wisdom of planning for our future? Of course, I do recom-mend making sure your goals are SMART (**s**pecific, **m**easur-able, **a**chievable, **r**elevant, and **t**ime-bound—see Appendix B). But my approach also offers three unique benefits beyond the usual best practices:

- Better quality of life through balancing your goals.
- Steady progress through following the 1–3–8–year rule and taking frequent action to achieve all your goals.
- Sustained motivation through reviewing and revising your goals at least every six months.

Balanced Goals, Balanced Life

The first unique feature of my approach is its emphasis on bal-anced goals. What do I mean by "balanced"? Like me, you have probably seen people successfully accomplish one goal at the expense of another—for example, achieving financial success while ignoring their physical health or sacrificing meaning-ful relationships. Then again, opting not to pay attention to your finances could also jeopardize your health or create a sig-nificant mental burden. Focusing too narrowly on one area of life while neglecting another can end in suffering and even tragedy.

Most of our goals are interrelated, so each will affect the others. This means we need to create goals that cover all the important areas of our life. This is achieved by setting up goals from the top down, beginning with our core beliefs and values (the "why" rather than the "what").

This doesn't have to be complicated. What are the areas of life that are important to you based on what you most deeply value? Do you want to develop brain power, muscle power, or both? Categorize those beliefs and values into four or five main groups and name them in whatever way works for you. I use four simple "central" goals that I then associate with "supportive" goals:

- Physical (health and fitness)
- Mental (education and travel)
- Social (relationships and friends)
- Financial (personal investing and career development)

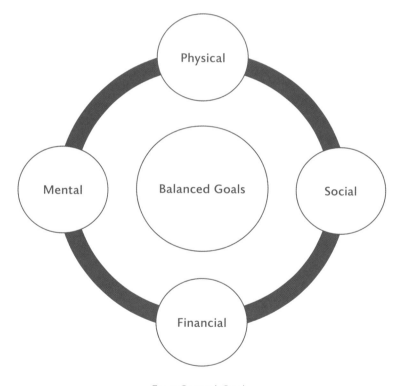

Four Central Goals

These central goals are the areas of life that are most important to me. You might want to change them or add other categories. For example, you might replace *mental* with *spiritual*, *physical* with *health,* financial with *wealth,* or *social* with *family.* The point is to create categories that make sense to you.

The supportive goals are, as the phrase suggests, more peripheral endeavors that indirectly support your central goals.

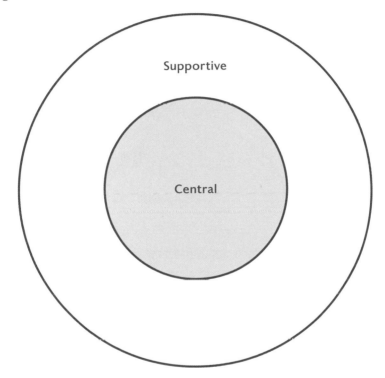

Two Levels of a Goal

For example, if your central mental goal is to finish a degree or complete a professional development course, a supportive mental goal might be to schedule in regular times to listen to music or read books.

A central physical goal to achieve a healthy body mass index or walk daily might have a supportive goal to work on your backyard.

A central social goal to organize a family gathering might have a supportive goal to look for higher-level connections. (See Appendix C for further examples of central and supportive goals.)

Below is an example of central and supportive financial goals.

Business investment planning

Residential rental property investment planning

Investment club

Land ownership

Budget

Debt reduction

Estate planning

Career

Tax planning

Home ownership

Personal investing

Partnership

Retirement planning

Commodity

Business rental

Commercial investment planning

An Example of Central and Supportive Goals

Make Steady Progress with the 1–3–8–Year Rule and Frequent Action

The duration of a goal is the time required to complete it. Why is it important to assign each goal a duration and completion date?

Without a completion date, a goal is just a dream.

- Knowing the completion date of your goals helps you know what to focus on at any given time as you work toward your goals.
- Knowing the completion date of all your goals motivates you to take action regularly to continue working toward them.
- By deciding what you want to accomplish and giving it a completion date, you will know what steps to take, and when to take them, so that you can meet your deadline.

I recommend categorizing your goals by my 1–3–8–year rule of short, medium, and long terms—but be flexible and do what makes sense for you. The idea of assigning time frames is meant to be helpful, not dogmatic.

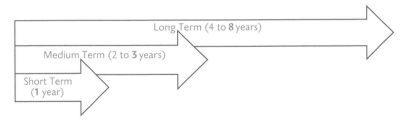

Short-term goals: Carried out and completed within one year. A year is a common milestone, and you can usually predict the critical variables fairly accurately for a one-year goal.

Reducing your weight to attain a more ideal body mass index is an example of a one-year goal.

Medium-term goals: Carried out and completed within one to three years. Although the time frame of these goals is still foreseeable, unpredicted variables are more likely to affect their completion than short-term goals. Writing this book was a medium-term goal I set up and completed within three years.

Long-term goals: Carried out and completed within three to eight years (or longer). With a longer duration, a goal's success will be affected by many unforeseen variables (the future is hard to predict). Thus, setting super-long-term goals of more than eight years is not practical. Long-term goals generally include milestones for evaluating their completion. Some long-term goals are made up of connected, short-term or medium-term goals. For example, before I started to work on my doctoral degree, I was required to submit a program of study listing the titles of all the required core and specialization courses and research seminars, as well as the number of hours of academic residencies. While the overall goal of getting my degree had a long-term completion of eight years, each course had its own three-month beginning and end dates, in succession. That is how you eat an elephant—one bite at a time![40]

An essential part of my goal-setting approach is to make sure you are taking action on goals of each duration consistently. This means you will be concurrently implementing all of your goals, taking action on them right from their starting date. Any delay in starting to act on a goal suggests it is still a wish. If you find you are not getting started, move the goal back to your wish list and reactivate it when you are ready to launch into action.

If you put off your long-term goals, you will not make long-term progress. This book is a good example of the value of an early start. Three years before my book's first printing, I started thinking about it regularly and making notes. Now and then, I went to the library to write. It was a slow start, but what matters is that I *started*.

That first year, I created a framework and wrote a chapter at a time. In the second year, I worked more diligently. Eventually, I was working on the book every day, quite intensively in the final months.

Over these years, my book expanded from a brief description of my goal-setting method to include my guidelines and life story. This evolution was possible only because I started on my goal immediately and worked on it frequently.

Update Your Goals to Strengthen Your Motivation

In my guidelines, I warn against the harm we can do to ourselves by comparing ourselves with others. The healthy alternative is to compare ourselves with our own past actions and future aspirations.

Have you made progress? Are you becoming who you want to be? Are you a better person now? Reviewing and updating your goals is a way to reenergize yourself through constructive self-comparison.

Life is dynamic and full of ups and downs. "Change is the only constant." This is another reason to update and revise our goals: to adapt to new challenges and situations. For example, before I emigrated, I deleted all my short-term goals and created new goals that would be more appropriate for my new life in the United States. One of these new goals was to get a driver license and buy a car. I had no need to drive in Hong Kong, but when I was living in the U.S., I would need my own transportation.

All goals should be reevaluated periodically to align with life's continuous changes. I recommend that all written goals be reviewed and revised:

- Near your birthday and six months before your next.
- When you are faced with an important life event (getting married, a new career, the birth of a child, etc.).
- When you are making a major decision (a large investment, getting ready to retire, preparing for a major move, etc.).
- At times when you need some inspiration.

When you perform a periodic review and revision of your goals, the duration of some of them may change. As long-term goals get closer to three years from their completion date, they become medium-term goals. When medium-term goals are down to a completion time of less than one year, change them to short-term goals.

For example, let's say you set up a goal to lose 10 pounds over two years. When a year has passed, and you have less than a year remaining, your goal now changes from being a medium- to a short-term goal.

While there may be situations where you must defer the starting date of a short-term goal, it should not be converted to a medium-term goal but should still be classified as short term.

This updating of completion dates is a vital part of your six-month reviews. If you don't move up your medium- and long-term goals over time, they will remain unaccomplished.

This six-month review is not something to do in a single sitting. Rather, it is an ongoing process to begin as early as a month before, or as late as a day before, its scheduled date, a bit like preparing for Christmas or another festival. Once you get into the habit of doing these regular reviews, the closer you get to review time, the more your thoughts will turn to your goals.

I find my birthday is the easier cue, because it is naturally on my mind. The challenge is following up six months later, so I mark this date on my calendar to remind myself that it is again time to revise, fine-tune, and update my goals. This has become something automatic for me, like a seasonal cycle. You will need to find your own ways of scheduling and prompting these reviews.

In addition to your six-month reviews, revisit your goals any time you feel down and need motivation. During my hardship years, when I felt low, I would sit down and review my goals and accomplishments. I would be reminded not only of my past successes, but of all I had to look forward to. I may have sat down discouraged, but I would get up feeling energized and recharged, ready to take action.

Put Your Goals in Writing

One of the most important things you can do to achieve your goals is to write them down. I know it sounds simple, but I assure you that written goals are powerful. Writing out a goal in your own words is what distinguishes it from a wish or dream. Tracking and updating your goals is possible only when you write them down. Even if you cannot accomplish all your goals, merely stating them in writing and revisiting them is motivating.

For decades now, I have kept written records of all my goals along with my accomplishments and other relevant facts about my life. At first I kept all this in a three-ring binder, divided into sections according to my central categories and past, present, and future. Eventually, I brought together a bounty of material representing all the important areas of my life. I also kept my wish lists and goal-setting statements in this binder.

As digital technologies developed, I moved my records onto the computer. I now use Excel spreadsheets. (Read more about how to set up these valuable goal-related records in Appendix D: Preparation for Goal Setting.)

It doesn't matter whether you use a binder (as I did in the early years) or computer software like Excel (as I do now), but you do want one crucial feature in whatever method you choose for tracking your goals: the ability to shuffle things around.

You need to be able to move your goals from your wish list to their appropriate duration and then to your list of accomplishments. So, find your own system, but make sure it allows you this flexibility to move things around and add new information over time.

Four Steps for Setting Your Goals: Why, What, How, and When?

I follow the same process when I'm setting up any major personal goal. My basic method involves answering four questions and turning the answers into a goal statement I can use to track and update that goal—first by clarifying what I want and then by guiding my actions—as I make progress toward achieving it.

The questions I use to help me outline my goal are why, what, how, and when:

- Why do I want to set up this goal?
- What do I want to achieve?

- How will I carry this out?
- When do I want to begin and complete the goal?

My method is similar to how you would plan a trip or vacation. When you think about going on a trip, your desire (your "why") is what drives the plan. Maybe you want to visit family, experience a different culture, or just relax. Driven by that desire, you choose the destination (your "what") and means of travel (your "how"), and review your calendar to find a suitable date and duration (your "when").

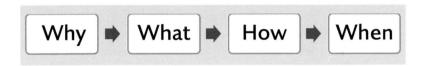

Below are examples of using the four questions to outline three different goals:

(a) Planning a journey
(b) Saving for a down payment on a house
(c) Earning a graduate degree

Why?

Almost all goals are driven by desires. Your "why" is what gives your goal meaning and gives you the "legs" needed to carry it out.

(a) *You are planning your journey because . . .*
- You have always had a desire to explore Europe.
- You are thrilled by the prospect of new adventures.
- You know travel will expand your awareness and offer an education you can't get from books.

Without the eagerness, planning your journey will seem like a chore and your journey might never happen.

(b) *You are planning to save for a down payment on a house because . . .*
- You want to pay your own mortgage rather than somebody else's.
- You are excited about the pride that comes with home ownership.
- You recognize the huge potential of investment return from real property.

Without enthusiasm for home ownership, saving money will feel like a daunting sacrifice.

(c) *You are planning to earn a graduate degree because . . .*
- You want the prestige of holding an advanced degree.
- You see the power this degree holds for the future of your career.
- You want to fulfill your lifelong academic goal of having an advanced degree.

Without the passion, attending classes will just be a long, drawn-out mental burden.

What?

Write a clear and exact statement to describe precisely *what* you want to achieve.

(a) *In planning your journey . . .* select a destination.

Without an end point, you cannot make all the necessary arrangements.

(b) *In planning to save for a down payment on a house . . .* figure out the amount you need.

Without the end number, you can't know how much to save each month.

(c) In *planning to earn a graduate degree* . . . choose a major.

Without naming a field of study, you're not able to focus your passion on a single area.

How?

Draw up a detailed plan to define *how* you will evaluate the goal. This plan will become the measurement instrument you need to track the progress of your goal.

(a) In *planning your journey* . . . prepare a detailed schedule.

Without an itinerary, the journey will likely derail.

(b) In *planning to save for a down payment on a house* . . .
create and stick to a monthly budget. Set aside a predetermined amount each month.

Without a monthly number, you won't accumulate the targeted funds by your completion date.

(c) In *planning to earn a graduate degree* . . . follow a specific program of study.

Without a full picture of the curriculum, you won't know how to complete the requirements for graduation.

When?

Write a precise timeline for *when* you want to carry out the goal. The starting time is more important than the completing time. At the risk of repeating myself, I'll remind you that without a time commitment to begin, the goal is still only a dream.

(a) In *planning your journey* . . . choose a time to go.

Without a specific date, the journey never happens.

(b) In *planning to save for a down payment on a house* . . . decide when you would like to be a homeowner.

Without a target date, you won't be able to calculate how much money you need to save regularly.

(c) *In planning to earn a graduate degree* ... set up a schedule
with application steps and course dates.
Without a schedule, you will never get started.

Goal Statements

WHEN YOU SET out on a journey, you need a map to help you navigate to your destination. Goal statements are maps for your life journey. They spell out the specific motivation, action steps, and timing you need to turn your wishes and dreams into concrete achievements. What's more, sitting down to create a goal statement using the four steps and template below will also help you clarify and organize your thinking.

Remember, if you don't set goals, you are just drifting through life. Though you are probably setting goals without realizing it (such as when you are planning a vacation), I am challenging you now to be more structured in your approach. Once you turn a wish into a structured goal, you have a clear and detailed map you can follow to your desired end point—an efficient, effective pathway to success.

Using the Four Steps

If you follow the four steps of *why, what, how,* and *when,* you will be able to produce a clear and workable goal statement for all your major goals. (There's no need to go through this process for minor goals.) The written goal statement is your first step toward commitment. Here is an example of one of my medium-term goals, to publish a book:

- Why: Writing a book has always been something I've wanted to do, an accomplishment I would be most proud of.

- *What*: The book is divided into three parts. Part One records the events since I arrived in California. Part Two lists the guidelines I have been following. Part Three describes the goal-setting plan I have been using to successfully manage my life for over 40 years.
- *How*: Draft outlines. Review and organize notes on the guidelines and goal-setting plan. Draft Part One stories. Draft Part Two guidelines. Draft Part Three balanced goals. Add introductions to all three parts and their chapters. Write something every day, regardless of what else is happening. Seek help from professional writers.
- *When*: The final draft of all three parts to be completed within two years. The whole manuscript to be completed within three years—by the end of December 2017.

A Goal Statement Template[41]

Why is the goal important to you?

What is the goal?

How will the goal be evaluated?

When will the goal be completed?

Epilogue

Destiny is not a matter of chance; it is a matter of choice.
It is not a thing to be waited for, it is a thing to be achieved.
—WILLIAM JENNINGS BRYAN

LOOKING BACK over these 30-plus years, I realize I have been very lucky and privileged. Timing was usually in my favor. I met many right people at the right time. Many right opportunities showed up at the right time as well. I will never forget the people who helped me become the person I want to be. A Chinese proverb says, yen shuǐ sī yuan (when one drinks water, think of its source). Those wonderful people are always on my mind.

Throughout my journey of settling down as a new citizen, I made a lot of mistakes and was taken advantage of a number of times. I was starting a new life in the United States and most of the practices, systems, and customs were literally completely foreign to me. However, I learned that mistakes were truly educational. Great teaching moments came disguised as blunders. People who took advantage of me helped enlighten me (see "Forgiving is better than getting even," on page 127). *The Nine Simple Guidelines for an Enriched Life* in Part Two are the combined essence of the ideas I discovered through instructing Dale Carnegie courses and the lessons I learned after arriving in San Diego. These guidelines continue to help me maintain a positive mental attitude whenever I am facing headwinds.

We all carry the memory of negative experiences. Unresolved pain can hold us back, just as those two incidents from my late teens and early twenties caused me great sadness and loss of confidence. For many years, I sought ways to mentally erase these memories, until I learned to change my attitude, set positive goals, and take other steps to overcome them.

Though these incidents were devastating at the time, I see now that they helped shape who I am today. The results far exceeded my expectations when, rather than reacting negatively, I chose to take positive action to eradicate the mental burden (see "Responding is better than reacting," on page 113). Closure for these two incidents allowed me to move forward with great peace of mind. I am grateful to report that, not only did I find resolution, but the search for healing helped me conceive a few of my guidelines.

Prepare Your Tools Early

My advice to younger readers:
- Develop good hobbies and interests early.
- Associate with positive and smart people always.
- Take part in motivational gatherings and events often.
- Save as much as you can regularly.
- Acquire broader areas of knowledge continually.

The time and effort invested in these activities will pay big dividends later in your life. Some of them may even be critical success factors that end up radically improving your life. Your hobby may turn out to be a crucial job skill for your future career. The smart people you associate with may influence you to become a better person. Inspiration from motivational events may offer you a different outlook on your life. When a great investment opportunity arises, you may well have accumulated sufficient funds to enhance your net worth.

Harvest won't happen unless you have collected and planted sufficient seeds first—the more one sows, the more one reaps. Our world is changing rapidly. Technology is making information so easily accessible. There is plenty of noise and misinformation all over the media. To differentiate between truth and delusion, you must keep learning.[42]

I've heard it said that "the best way to predict your future is to create it." You need tools in the form of skills, connections, enthusiasm, funds, and knowledge to shape your future.

It may be challenging to follow the role models of successful people. But it is so much easier to stay away from the harmful habits of failures. Success is merely failure turned inside out. Therefore, if you *don't* do the things failures do, you are giving yourself much better odds to become successful.[43]

Take Back Control of Your Life

Be the person you want to be, **never** what others want you to be!

I am the master of my fate;
I am the captain of my soul.
—WILLIAM ERNEST HENLEY

Appendix A
Decision Matrix Evaluating
Laptop Computers

THE FOLLOWING is an example of a decision matrix designed for selecting one of four laptop computers using five criteria with various weightings, or levels of importance. The processor is the most important consideration, assigned a weight of 5. The hard drive is the least important, assigned a weight of 1.

For each laptop, the score indicates how its features compare with the rest. For example, in a comparison of the four laptop models, the findings show that the processors of Laptops 1 and 4 are not as good as those of the others (given the score of 1), but Laptop 1's display is the best among all of them (given the score of 5).

Factor/Criteria	Weighting	Laptop 1	Laptop 2	Laptop 3	Laptop 4
Processor	5	1	3	5	1
Display	4	5	2	1	4
Memory	3	2	3	5	5
Price	2	3	4	2	4
Hard Drive	1	3	2	1	1
Simple Average Score		2.80	2.80	2.80	3.00
Weighted Average Score		2.67	2.80	3.27	3.00

A Decision Matrix to Evaluate Different Models of Laptop Computers

As shown in the matrix, the simple average score of Laptop 4 is the highest and the rest are identical. The weighted average score of Laptop 3 is the highest. If weights are included in the decision of selecting a laptop, then the choice should be Laptop 3.

A simple average score is calculated by dividing the sum of each component's assigned weighting number by the total number of components.

The simple average score of Laptop 1 =

$$(1+2+5+3+3)/5 = 14/5 = 2.80.$$

A weighted average score is calculated by first multiplying each component's assigned number by its weighting then dividing the result by the sum of the weighting numbers.

The weighted average score of Laptop 1 =

$$(1\times5+5\times4+2\times3+3\times2+3\times1)/(5+4+3+2+1) = 40/15 = 2.67.$$

Appendix B
Make Your Goals SMART

I F YOU'VE DONE any research on goal setting, you are probably familiar with the acronym SMART. This acronym helps us remember that a goal is SMART when it is:

Specific: A goal must be precise and have a clear outcome. Aim straight at the target by answering "What? Where? Why? With what people and resources?"

Measurable: A goal must be quantifiable so you can track your progress and stay motivated. Change words to numbers and answer the questions "How much? How many? How will I know when I'm finished?"

Achievable: A goal must be both challenging enough to spark your passion and realistic enough to complete—currently out of reach but not out of sight.

Relevant: A goal must align with your values and have an expected outcome worthy of your core beliefs.

Time-bound: A goal must have prompt times for starting and completion and be recognized as short, medium, or long term.

Appendix C
Goal-Planning Matrix

A GOAL-PLANNING matrix provides you with a high-level view of all your goals with a balanced perspective. You can easily create a matrix using a spreadsheet application such as Microsoft Excel. Once you have created a template, you can use it again and again.

In this example, I have mapped my four main goal categories (physical, mental, financial, and social) with their two levels (central and supportive) and three durations (short, medium, and long term).

The first matrix is my template. The second is an example of how I might fill in that template.

	Short Term	Medium Term	Long Term
Physical	*Central*	*Central*	*Central*
	Supportive	*Supportive*	*Supportive*
Mental	*Central*	*Central*	*Central*
	Supportive	*Supportive*	*Supportive*
Financial	*Central*	*Central*	*Central*
	Supportive	*Supportive*	*Supportive*
Social	*Central*	*Central*	*Central*
	Supportive	*Supportive*	*Supportive*

Goal-Planning Matrix: Template

	Short Term	Medium Term	Long Term
Physical	*Central* Walk 50 minutes, five times a week *Supportive* Work in backyard four times a week	*Central* Lose five pounds *Supportive* Learn a few yoga poses	*Central* Stick to a healthy diet *Supportive* Master the techniques of tai chi
Mental	*Central* Read one book every two months *Supportive* Look for job openings	*Central* Learn to speak and write basic Japanese *Supportive* Start a new hobby	*Central* Publish a book *Supportive* Keep learning something new
Financial	*Central* Monitor stock market daily *Supportive* Control monthly budget	*Central* Buy a new car *Supportive* Seek a new career	*Central* Buy a residential rental property *Supportive* Actively support one charitable organization
Social	*Central* Get together with family monthly *Supportive* Call or email three friends a week	*Central* Visit a few cities in Asia with family *Supportive* Reconnect with one old friend	*Central* Help a family member to buy a house *Supportive* Offer volunteer service to one charitable organization

Goal-Planning Matrix: Sample Content

Appendix D
Preparation for Goal Setting

To map a route to a destination, you must know from where you are starting and to where you are going. For the same reason, when you are designing a major goal, knowing where you are now will be crucial to planning for your future, as will analyzing your past.

As the saying goes, "Life is a journey, not a destination." Life's journey is made up of three phases: past, present, and future. The past is what you have already done, the present is where you are now, and your goals are about your future.

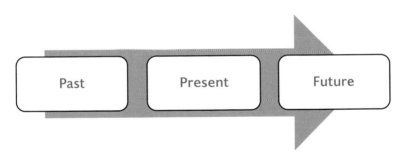

Past   Present   Future

Prior to setting up any major goals or revising existing goals, we need to know who we are and where we stand. Good planning requires a foundation of detailed analysis. Gathering information and up-to-date records about ourselves is necessary before we can work on the specifics of our goals.

Choose your own preferred format for storing and organizing your records. If you prefer paper records, you can design your own version of the sectioned three-ring binder I used when I first began keeping these records (see page 159).

You can also enter, organize, and manage detailed records using database or document-management software, such as Microsoft Excel.[44] Documents, photographs, and papers can be scanned and saved as digital files for easy reference and retrieval. This is the system I use today.

The process of setting up your system and gathering records for this analysis is not something to do in one or two sittings. It is a dynamic process that you will pick up, work on, and put down, again and again. Give yourself time.

You may want to begin by setting up the framework you want to use, either in a binder or on your computer. Decide in what core areas you will be setting goals. Then use the following instructions to make notes on what you want to collect. Let this be an organic process based on what goals you currently want to create.

For example, if your focus right now is on financial goals, you don't need to spend time gathering health records. Make it your priority to set up your financial information as set out below.

Analyzing the Past

The past can be analyzed from the records and recollections of your:
- Accomplishments
- Regrets
- Best practices

Accomplishments

Things you are proud of:
- Achievements
- Awards
- Special family and social gatherings
- Interesting experiences
- Letters and notes
- Collections of photo albums and digital pictures
- Places visited
- Recognitions
- Unique events attended

Regrets

Things you would do differently:
- Bad investments
- Erroneous opinions
- Opportunities missed
- People you treated unkindly
- Poor attitudes
- Wrong decisions

Best practices

Things you would do again:
- Good choices
- Profitable investments
- Valuable positive outcomes

Evaluating the Present

You can appraise your present by using the current detailed records of your main types of capital that constitute your total self-worth, such as:
  (a) Health status (your body capital)
  (b) Net worth (your financial capital)
  (c) Education, training, and qualifications (your knowledge capital)
  (d) Contacts (your relationship capital)

Health status (your body capital)

Medical records (include those of spouse and dependents)
  • Allergies
  • Conditions
  • Medications
  • Test results
  • Vitals

Net worth (your financial capital)

Financial assets
  • Automobiles
  • Bank accounts
  • Collections
  • Home equity
  • Investments
  • Jewelry

**Education, training, and qualifications
(your knowledge capital)**

Curriculum vitae (résumé)
- Certificates
- Diplomas
- Licenses
- List of experience
- Skills
- Transcripts
- Vocational training

Contacts (your relationship capital)

Families and social acquaintances (for each one)
- Name
- Company
- Address
- Email address
- Phone number

Deciding the Future

Goal setting for the future is all about making wishes. A record of things desired is commonly known as a wish list, dream list, or bucket list. Fantasize about your desires. You can get big results by thinking and believing in BIG.

Start a wish list by writing down:
- Things you would like to own
- Places you would like to visit
- People you would like to meet
- Challenges you would like to overcome
- Adventures you would like to experience
- Keep adding to your list whenever ideas or inspirations cross your mind, and review it when you are drafting or revising goals.

I encourage you to generate an extensive list of dreams and desires. Your wish list can serve as a powerful motivator.

Endnotes

Part One

1. S. Lee and F. Li. "Thatcher Praised by China for Ending U.K. Rule in Hong Kong," *Macau Daily Times* (April 9, 2013), macaudailytimes.com. mo/archive-2009–2014/china/42908-thatcher-praised-for-ending-uk-rule-in-hong-kong.html.

2. Read more about Hong Kong's drug rehabilitation island at tinyurl.com/acruzgg6.

3. See D. Carnegie, *How to Win Friends and Influence People* (Rev. ed.) (New York, NY: Simon & Schuster, 1981), 74.

4. Richard Eisenberg published a follow-up article on this book. See "30 Years Ago They Retired at 35: An Update," *Forbes*, tinyurl.com/acruzgg1.

5. Read about the Shanghai French Concession at tinyurl.com/acruzgg9.

6. Launched in 1927, the Chartered Life Underwriter (CLU) is the insurance profession's oldest standard of excellence. See tinyurl.com/acruzgg10.

7. From a small section of Social Security Benefit Worksheet Instructions of Internal Revenue Service Tax Form 1040 (U.S. Individual Income Tax Return).

8. For the history of ChipSoft and TurboTax, see tinyurl.com/acruzgg11.

9. The Motley Fool is at fool.com.

10. Information about Warren Buffet is from tinyurl.com/acruzgg3.

11. My master's thesis, a literature review on the prevention of child sexual abuse, was research conducted on behalf of the End Child Sexual Abuse Foundation (ecsaf.org.hk), where I am an honorary advisor.

12. Inspired by Joan Bolker, *Writing Your Dissertation in Fifteen Minutes a Day: A Guide to Starting, Revising, and Finishing Your Doctoral Thesis* (New York: Henry Holt and Company, 1998).

13. The transcript of Bill Clinton's graduation speech is available at tinyurl.com/acruzgg4.

14. Albert Cruz Park is located at 611 West Melrose Drive, Casa Grande, Arizona 85122.

15. Learn more about Disneyland's private club at disneylandclub33.com.

16. The hotel from which I last spoke to my dad is Keio Plaza Hotel Tokyo, 2-2-1 Nishi-Shinjuku, Shinjuku-Ku, Tokyo, 160-8330 Japan.

17. San Diego Mesa College is the largest of three colleges in the San Diego Community College District (sdccd.edu/about/index.aspx).

18. Mount San Jacinto College is online at msjc.edu.

19. Inspired by Chris Guillebeau, *The Happiness of Pursuit: Finding the Quest that Will Bring Purpose to Your Life* (New York: Harmony Books, 2014).

Part Two

20. Millennials might be interested in this more recent version: Dale Carnegie & Associates, *How to Win Friends and Influence People in the Digital Age* (New York: Simon & Schuster, 2011).

21. Try a Kia comparison commercial: https://youtu.be/eudVDoAaTiw.

22. For simplicity, the amount for one week is equal to the monthly amount divided by four, and the amount for one day is equal to the monthly amount divided by 30.

23. zenhabits.net.

24. Y. Lin, *The Importance of Living* (New York, NY: William Morrow and Company, 1937).

25. With the development of information technology, many organizations use data analytics to augment the effectiveness of their operations.

26. Frank E. Sullivan was a founder of the University of Notre Dame's lay board of trustees and the author of *The Critical Path to Sales Success* (N.p.: Research and Review Service of America, 1970).

27. As illustrated by the Fibonacci sequence: 0, 1, 1, 2, 3, 5, 8, 13, 21, 34, 55, 89 . . .

28. See the Rube Goldberg Gallery at rubegoldberg.com.

29. Thomas Buser and Noemi Peter, "Multitasking," *Experimental Economics* 15 (2012), doi: 10.1007/s10683-012-9318-8.

30. tinyurl.com/acruzgg5.

31. coachwooden.com.

32. D. Zhang, *Key Concepts in Chinese Philosophy*, trans. Edmund Ryden (New Haven, CT: Yale University Press, 2002).

33. Source: J. Rowley, "The Wisdom Hierarchy: Representations of the DIKW Hierarchy," *Journal of Information Science* 33, no. 2 (2007): 163–180, doi: 10.1177/0165551506070706.

34. sirkenrobinson.com.

35. See tinyurl.com/acruzgg12.

36. See tinyurl.com/acruzgg14.

37. See tinyurl.com/acruzgg13.

38. Mind-mapping is to brainstorm thoughts organically without worrying about order and structure. See mindmapping.com/mind-map.php.

39. mindtools.com.

Part Three

40. See B. Hogan, *How Do You Eat an Elephant? One Bite at a Time* (Coral Springs, FL: Llumina Press, 2004) and J. Parker, *How to Eat an Elephant: How to Tackle Any Challenge…and Succeed* (St. Albans, UK: Ecademy Press, 2011).

41. A digital copy of this statement is available at hk2-usa.com.

42. O.Benson and J. Stangroom, *Why Truth Matters* (London: Continuum, 2006).

43. Inspired by Albert E.N. Gray's words: "The common denominator of success—the secret of every man who has ever been successful—lies in the fact that he formed the habit of doing things that failures don't like to do."

44. For an assessment of document-management software options, see tinyurl.com/acruzgg2.

Chronology

1982   Shocked by the sudden death of Dad
Disturbed by the uncertainty of the future of
   Hong Kong

1983   Arrived in San Diego with family as new immigrants
Learned how to drive

1984   Started Acanda Insurance Services, Inc.

1985   Began instructing Dale Carnegie course
Completed my first U.S. tax return

1986   Went through financial hardship
Worked as a laborer at jobs assigned by a temp agency
Recognized the true value of money

1987   Bought a condo to live in

1988   Completed San Diego International Marathon

1989   Became a citizen of the United States
Received Dale Carnegie Leadership award

1990   Bought several residential rental properties

1991   Prepared taxes at H&R Block
Closed down Acanda Insurance Services, Inc.

1992   Bought a single-family house, which I named *The First
Step*, at Poway
Started as a part-time QA tester at ChipSoft (later
acquired by Intuit)

1993   Began full-time employment at Intuit

1994   Became a Tax Analyst Programmer at Intuit

1997   Hong Kong was handed over to China

1998   Began college
Qualified as an Enrolled Agent of the IRS

2000	Attended Berkshire Hathaway's annual meeting of shareholders
	Completed a BS degree in information systems
2002	Completed an MBA degree in technology management
	Gave a commencement speech at San Diego Convention Center
	Retired from Intuit
2003	Started teaching part-time at National University
2005	Completed an MA degree in human behavior
	Bought a single-family house, which I named *The Second Step*, at Rancho Bernardo
2007	Became a full-time faculty at National University
	Escaped from Rancho Bernardo wildfire
2008	First visit to Hong Kong in 18 years
2009	Presented a paper at a conference in Jeju Island, South Korea
2011	Completed a doctoral degree in knowledge management
2012	Retired for the second time
2013	Moved to Riverside County
	Started teaching part-time at San Diego Mesa College
2015	Began writing this book

Acknowledgments

I WOULD LIKE TO express my gratitude in memory of my beloved Mom, Ruby, who scored high marks on all four balanced goals I describe in Part Three of this book. A lifelong learner with very little formal education, she was cordial with friends, wonderful with relatives, and kind to her children and grandchildren. Mom enjoyed a long and healthy life free of any financial worries. We all miss her.

My heartfelt thanks to my wife, Teresa, and our daughters, Janette and Mary-Ann, who stood by me while we were going through the challenges of a fresh start in the United States over 30 years ago. Together, we walked toward a new frontier with little knowledge of what lay ahead.

The Chinese believe it can be very rewarding if one is fortunate enough to meet a *noble person* (guì rén) in the right place and at the right time. My life would not have been as fulfilled had I not come across such *noble persons* at various junctures of my path. Each of them gave me critical support and influenced me, and so contributed to many of my life's major positive turning points.

It has been a privilege to be acquainted with the following extraordinary people to whom I would like to give special recognition:

Thurman, Warren, and Clarke Hewitt, three exceptional brothers, for offering their unconditional help to Mom and to my family.

Connie and Julius Ng, a wonderful couple we knew before we immigrated, for sustaining our friendship for nearly four decades.

Don and Phil Goode, two superb insurance brokers, for their gracious efforts and professionalism in helping me set up my insurance business.

Betty and Raymond Fong, our first Chinese friends in California, for extending a helping hand to me and my family throughout the low point of our early years in California.

Jennifer and Jim Metzger, a fantastic couple who were neighbors at the first condo we owned, for being our best American friends. Jim was my running mate during my marathon training.

Mike Crom, a personable manager of Dale Carnegie Institute at San Diego, for accepting me as an instructor even though English is my second language and I had no college degree.

The amazing class members of the Dale Carnegie courses I instructed in Hong Kong and in the United States for enlightening me with their wisdom and teaching me about their culture.

Bill Shepard, a former manager of the Professional Tax Group at Intuit, for giving me (a person with only a foreign high school diploma) the terrific opportunity to become a member of the elite Development Team of TurboTax.

John Bugado, a supportive department chair of Computer Science and Information Systems at National University in San Diego, for helping me achieve my goal of having a faculty career in academia. Teaching has always been my passion.

Dr. Suki Stone, a passionate doctoral degree mentor, for coaching me to successfully complete my dissertation.

Dr. Amber Lo, a good friend and a great colleague at National University, for giving me valuable input and advice on the final draft of this book.

Virginia Law, a brilliant business partner, for conscientiously managing—over three decades—the company I founded in Hong Kong. The uninterrupted dividends were crucial to my survival during the hardship years, and later those dividends aided me greatly in building a solid financial foundation.

I would also like to thank Janette Cruz, Mary-Ann Cruz, Wendy Eng-Rytell, and Cynthia Williams for reviewing and providing supportive comments on the draft chapters of this book.

Finally, Dave Rytell, a dear and learned friend, for sharing his perceptions and wisdom. Dave inspired me to pursue higher education while we were colleagues at Intuit. Most notably, with Dave's help, the publication of this book became a reality rather than a dream.

To My Reader

December 2017
(my 34th Anniversary of "coming to the U.S.")

To My Reader,

Writing this book has been a great joy for me. Many years ago, I had a desire to write down a few ideas about how I overcame my life's challenges and successfully implemented my goal-setting plan. I postponed this endeavor when I went back to full-time study, but as soon as I had completed my doctoral degree, I got down to it as one of my medium-term mental goals.

Over the past three years, I put my heart and soul into recollecting the highlights from four decades of my life. I organized my notes on the guidelines and rearranged materials on goal setting. I was also fortunate that many friends and professional writers agreed to review the manuscript and offer suggestions to help refine my work.

If you come across any message that inspires you—even if you find just one useful or helpful idea—this will make all the effort and resources I invested in this book well worthwhile.

I do wish you all the best in becoming who you want to be. Keep saving, learning, exercising, and loving.

Sincerely,

Albert Cruz

Menifee, California

Website: hk2-usa.com
Facebook: @becomingwhoyouwanttobe
Twitter: #ACruzBecomingMe

Index